The Golden Age of Speed

Motorsport in the 1950s and 60s

Etienne Psaila

The Golden Age of Speed: Motorsport in the 1950s and 60s

Copyright © 2024 by Etienne Psaila. All rights reserved.

First Edition: **December 2024**

No part of this publication may be reproduced, distributed, or transmitted in any form or by any means, including photocopying, recording, or other electronic or mechanical methods, without the prior written permission of the publisher, except in the case of brief quotations embodied in critical reviews and certain other non-commercial uses permitted by copyright law.

ISBN: 978-1-923393-31-8

Table of Contents

1. Introduction: Defining the Golden Age
2. Racing Reborn: The Post-War Context
3. The Titans of the Early 1950s
4. Ascendancy of the British and the Mid-Engine Revolution
5. The New Wave of 1960s Driving Icons
6. Formula One's Coming of Age
7. Europe's Legendary Circuits and Classic Grands Prix
8. Sports Car Racing and Endurance Battles
9. The American Scene: Indy, USAC, and NASCAR
10. Cross-Pollination of Ideas: Europe Meets America
11. Mechanical Marvels: Engineering and Design Breakthroughs
12. Safety on the Edge: Dangers and Disasters
13. Rivalries and National Pride
14. Commercialization and the Start of Sponsorship
15. Media, Glamour, and Celebrity Culture
16. The Role of Privateers and Gentleman Racers
17. Underrepresented Stories: Women and Minorities in Racing
18. Tuning and Mechanics: The Unsung Heroes of the Paddock
19. Shifts in Driving Ethos and Professionalism
20. The Winds of Change: Late 1960s Transitions

Epilogue: Legacy of the Golden Age
Appendix: Photo Gallery

1. Introduction: Defining the Golden Age

In the years immediately following the Second World War, a profound sense of possibility began to radiate across Europe, North America, and beyond. Much of the world had emerged from a period defined by deprivation and conflict, and now the focus turned to rebuilding economies, reestablishing international trade, and rediscovering cultural pastimes that had been put on hold. Into this fertile ground stepped motorsport, a spectacle that promised speed, innovation, and transcendent heroes during a time of renewal and hope.

By the late 1940s, new racing events were being organized with growing enthusiasm, and pre-war circuits were restored to host them. The scars of war were still visible in places like Monza's aging grandstands or the roads of the Nürburgring region, but spectators returned in droves, hungry for the excitement they had been denied for so long. Automakers, spurred by the urgent need to rebuild their reputations and engage global markets, once again invested time and resources into competitive racing programs. In this environment of open roads and fresh ideas, motorsport became a vivid arena in which technology, skill, and national pride could freely mix.

What emerged in the 1950s and 1960s was a unique era, often called the golden age of motorsport. It was an age when cars were evolving at breakneck speed, when a handful of daring individuals—some trained engineers, others instinctual geniuses—turned the driver's seat into a cockpit of drama and danger. From the Grand Prix circuits of Europe to the endurance tests of the Le Mans 24 Hours, from the dusty ovals of America's heartland to the twisting roads of the Targa Florio in Sicily, the sport flourished in unprecedented ways.

This wasn't merely about speed records or the introduction of new mechanical components. It was about a genuine cultural moment. Drivers from across the globe, many of whom began their careers in modified road cars, became international celebrities. Magazines, newspapers, and eventually television broadcasts brought these figures into living rooms, inspiring a new generation of fans who admired both the glamour and the nerve it took to compete. Racing teams—led by inventive minds like Enzo Ferrari, Alfred Neubauer, and later Colin Chapman—rose to household-name status, and the cars they created were as admired for their engineering brilliance as for their sleek designs.

The term "golden age" is often used to describe a time that seems larger than life in retrospect, and the motorsport scene of the 1950s and 1960s fits this description for several reasons. First, this was an era marked by rapid technological progress that remained visibly human. Drivers could still be seen wrestling with steering wheels in cars that had little in the way of aerodynamic wings or electronic aids. Engineers could experiment, sometimes radically, and innovations like disc brakes, mid-engine layouts, and space-frame chassis were tested not in secret but in front of a growing, captivated audience.

Second, the racing world had not yet fragmented into the highly specialized forms that dominate today. In these decades, many drivers crossed disciplinary lines—

competing in Formula One one week and a major endurance race the next, sometimes tackling the Indianapolis 500 or even dabbling in sports car rallies. The result was a richly interconnected racing tapestry, with no single series entirely overshadowing the others.

Finally, there was the atmosphere. Circuits like Monza, Spa-Francorchamps, and the Nürburgring Nordschleife still followed their older, perilous layouts. The gravel run-offs were minimal, the guardrails often improvised, and the danger inherent in racing added a dramatic tension that, for better or worse, is central to the era's mystique. Although tragic accidents would later compel fundamental changes in safety standards, at the time this inherent risk was inseparable from the sport's identity—and part of what made its participants so revered.

In truth, hindsight can lend a certain romance to the past, but the factual developments of the 1950s and 1960s support this notion of a golden age. Records were broken at a furious pace, new teams and cars emerged from all corners of the globe, and whole industries grew around the pursuit of speed. Motorsports in these decades linked old-world craftsmanship with the dawn of the space age, reflecting broader cultural shifts. This was an era where one might see a Maserati's handcrafted engine face off against a British Cooper's pioneering rear-engine configuration, or an American V8 challenge a refined Italian V12, all in front of a chorus of international spectators.

As we venture deeper into the chapters that follow, we will explore these transformative years in detail. We will meet the drivers who defied the odds, the engineers who thought beyond conventional boundaries, the circuits that became testing grounds for human and machine, and the evolving values of a society grappling with modernity. Above all, we will witness how, for a brief, shining period, motorsport captured the global imagination—becoming as much an expression of art and national identity as it was a contest of speed. This is the story of why the 1950s and 1960s remain, even decades later, a golden benchmark against which every subsequent racing era is measured.

2. Racing Reborn: The Post-War Context

In the winter-chilled ruins of post-war Europe, as economies lay fractured and communities struggled to regain their footing, a quiet but determined effort began to revive motorsport. Before the conflict, Grand Prix racing and long-distance road competitions had already achieved a certain grandeur—cars and drivers were national icons, and great races like the Monaco Grand Prix, the Mille Miglia, and the 24 Hours of Le Mans had cultivated passionate audiences. But from 1939 onward, the roar of racing engines fell silent across battle-torn continents. Circuits were left untended or repurposed for military use, manufacturing shifted solely to wartime needs, and the international rivalries once played out on the track were replaced by very real and devastating conflicts of arms.

When the war ended in 1945, the world faced a monumental task of rebuilding. Cities rose from rubble, factories retooled for peace, and families struggled to restore normalcy. In this atmosphere, the reemergence of motorsport stood as a symbol of renewal and hope. For many, the return of racing offered a glimpse into a more vibrant, forward-looking era, tapping into a universal craving for entertainment, healthy competition, and technological progress.

The process began at a grassroots level. Some of the first post-war competitions were modest and locally organized, meant more to rekindle interest than to set records. Airfields, no longer needed for military sorties, were converted into improvised racetracks. In Britain, for instance, the former Royal Air Force base at Silverstone became the setting for a new generation of British Grands Prix, starting in 1948. Across Europe, circuits like Monza in Italy or Spa-Francorchamps in Belgium, which had fallen quiet for years, were gradually repaired and prepared for spectators. The reintroduction of classic events—Le Mans resumed in 1949 and the Targa Florio was revived in 1948—signaled that the traditions of pre-war racing could be reclaimed.

Economic conditions improved steadily throughout the late 1940s and into the 1950s. The Marshall Plan in Europe injected funds into reconstruction, and industrial output rose quickly. Increasing prosperity meant that manufacturers could invest once again in motorsport, not just as a marketing exercise, but as a field laboratory for testing engineering innovations. Races had always doubled as proving grounds for reliability and performance, and after the war, the lessons learned in industrial design, lightweight materials, and engine technologies filtered back into the racing sphere. Ferrari, Alfa Romeo, Maserati, and later British marques like Cooper and BRM, recognized that competition could drive better engineering—a philosophy shared by emerging teams in Germany and France as well.

International cooperation also began to reshape the racing landscape. The Fédération Internationale de l'Automobile (FIA) took steps to formalize a set of regulations and a championship structure, culminating in the launch of the official Formula One World Championship in 1950. This step was crucial: it brought together top drivers and manufacturers under a recognized framework, channeling global attention on a series of races rather than isolated events. For the first time, a driver could be crowned "World Champion," heightening the stakes and intrigue.

In North America, the United States saw a post-war economic boom that helped seed its own vibrant motorsport culture. The Indianapolis Motor Speedway reopened with a triumphant revival of the Indianapolis 500 in 1946, continuing a tradition that had paused during the war. Meanwhile, NASCAR—founded in 1948—built on regional stock car racing traditions and quickly found a national audience ready for thrilling, door-to-door battles on high-banked ovals. Like Europe, America's newfound prosperity supported the growth of racing into a professional sport, beloved by spectators who increasingly had the disposable income and leisure time to attend events in person.

Taken together, these developments formed the backbone of a motorsport revival that stretched across continents. Old circuits were reinvigorated, international competitions were reestablished, and the broadening of technical regulations inspired a flurry of engineering creativity. The late 1940s and early 1950s marked a collective turning point—racing was no longer the domain of a few hardy enthusiasts; it was becoming an integral part of post-war cultural recovery and pride.

Newspapers of the time covered major events with enthusiastic detail, chronicling the return of famous drivers and heralding the arrival of rising talent. Spectators, whether gathered at local tracks or poring over race reports in magazines, sensed something special was afoot: motorsport was not just coming back—it was growing into something more complex, more competitive, and more widely celebrated than ever before.

This broad base of support, fueled by economic upswing and bolstered by the memory of what had been lost during the war, ensured that the stage was set for a transformation. As the 1950s dawned, fans and participants alike sensed that they were on the threshold of a period in racing history that would blend tradition with innovation, and endurance with elegance. With the heavy weight of recent history still close at hand, the burgeoning motorsport world stood poised to redefine itself, setting the stage for the golden age that lay just ahead.

3. The Titans of the Early 1950s

By the dawn of the 1950s, a new chapter in motor racing was well underway, and at its center stood a group of drivers whose prowess, style, and rivalry helped shape the sport's early narrative. These men were not just competitors; they were national icons, ambassadors of their manufacturers' pride, and figures who embodied the evolving nature of post-war Grand Prix racing. Among the most celebrated of these early titans were Juan Manuel Fangio, Giuseppe "Nino" Farina, Alberto Ascari, and Mike Hawthorn.

Giuseppe Farina

The honor of becoming the first-ever Formula One World Champion in 1950 fell to Giuseppe Farina, an Italian driver of cultivated manner and resolute driving style. Farina's approach behind the wheel combined intellect with aggression: he was known to favor deliberate lines and believed deeply in the value of physical fitness, which he credited for his edge during long, grueling races. Driving for Alfa Romeo, he managed to outpace his formidable teammate, Juan Manuel Fangio, in that inaugural championship. He fused the pre-war traditions of racing—where technical skill and courage mattered above all—with the post-war age's demand for consistent, measured performance. Farina's triumphs, even before Formula One's official codification, set the tone for the sport's seriousness and sophistication. He was an early embodiment of the "complete driver," one who recognized that success in this new world required both flair and calculated discipline.

Juan Manuel Fangio

If Farina's 1950 title announced the post-war era, it was Juan Manuel Fangio who would soon take it by the reins and lead it into its prime. The Argentine driver, often hailed as the greatest of his generation, claimed an astonishing five World Championships between 1951 and 1957, a record that would stand for decades. Fangio's skill lay not only in his remarkable adaptability—he raced and won in Alfa Romeo, Mercedes-Benz, Ferrari, and Maserati cars—but also in his profound mechanical sympathy. Known for his uncanny sense of mechanical limits, Fangio never seemed to overtax his equipment. He understood the machine beneath him with a craftsman's instinct, coaxing the best from it without pushing it toward failure. Watching Fangio at the wheel, observers saw smoothness and fluidity, a refined style that spared his tires and engine while allowing him to maintain staggering pace. His fearless overtakes, strategic thinking, and the respect he commanded from teammates and rivals alike elevated him to a level of near-mythic status in the paddock.

Alberto Ascari

For a time, however, there was a man who could rival Fangio in sheer dominance: Alberto Ascari, the quiet Italian who brought Ferrari to the forefront of motorsport's consciousness. Ascari clinched consecutive World Championships in 1952 and 1953, years in which his near-total supremacy was underscored by an unmatched consistency. Ascari's genius lay in his precision: he was methodical, smooth, and unwaveringly consistent, qualities that paired perfectly with Ferrari's evolving machinery. He reeled off strings of victories that defined the early years of the championship, his cockpit demeanor calm and his trajectories exact. While Fangio was lauded for adapting to various cars, Ascari honed his craft with Ferrari, forging a near-symbiotic relationship with the red machines of Maranello. His success raised the bar for everyone else, demonstrating that mastery of a specific car and a methodical approach to racing could prove just as mighty as Fangio's mechanical empathy and adaptability.

Mike Hawthorn

Across the English Channel, British racing fans found their first real Grand Prix superstar in Mike Hawthorn. Debonair, and often sporting his trademark bow tie, Hawthorn was representative of Britain's rising engineering and driving capabilities in the 1950s. He contested fiercely against the continental giants, ultimately securing the 1958 World Championship and becoming Britain's first Formula One title winner. While his championship year lies just beyond the early 1950s bracket, Hawthorn's presence was already felt in that formative era. Known for his bravery, he could be aggressive at the wheel and excelled under pressure—an attribute that came to define the British involvement in the sport. His rivalry with drivers like Fangio occurred on legendary circuits—Spa, the Nürburgring, Reims—where his combination of daring and technical acuity earned him respect. Though Hawthorn's life and career were tragically short, his success signaled that Grand Prix racing was becoming a truly international battleground, no longer the sole domain of Italians, Argentines, or Germans.

Rivalries and Championships

As the 1950s advanced, these titans clashed at circuits that tested both man and machine. The early championship years often featured Fangio and Ascari trading wins race after race, each probing for the other's weaknesses. The spectacle of these contests, watched from grassy embankments and makeshift stands around Europe, helped cement Formula One as a premier global sporting attraction. Farina's early triumphs faded somewhat as Ascari and Fangio rose to prominence, but his role as the trailblazer of the championship was never forgotten. Later, the arrival of Hawthorn and other British contenders began to reshape the grid, adding new dimensions of rivalry, car design philosophies, and racing tactics.

Each of these early champions had a distinct style: Fangio's fluid adaptability, Ascari's metronomic consistency, Farina's disciplined aggression, and Hawthorn's spirited daring. Their achievements and battles defined the first true championship era of Grand Prix racing. They laid the groundwork upon which subsequent legends would build—setting standards for technical understanding, racecraft, and courage that still resonate in the sport's collective memory today.

They were the Titans of the early 1950s, guiding motorsport

into a golden age where the pursuit of speed, engineering excellence, and personal glory formed an irresistible narrative for spectators around the world. Their legacies remain intertwined with the very essence of what made racing's mid-century period so compelling.

4. Ascendancy of the British and the Mid-Engine Revolution

By the late 1950s, the center of gravity in Grand Prix racing began to shift in a way that would reshape the sport's future. For much of the early decade, Formula One machinery followed a familiar pattern: powerful engines mounted at the front, driving the rear wheels through transmissions that had evolved steadily from pre-war designs. Yet hidden away in small workshops and garages across England were a handful of engineers and innovators who saw the sport differently. They believed in a radical concept—placing the engine behind the driver—and this idea would ignite a revolution.

The earliest flicker of this change came from the Cooper Car Company, a small British constructor led by Charles and John Cooper. Initially successful in junior formulae, the Coopers had taken notice of the advantages mid- and rear-engine layouts offered in lightweight racing cars. The reasoning was simple enough: relocating the engine to the rear could improve weight distribution, lower the car's center of gravity, and enhance handling in corners. The Coopers brought this philosophy into Formula One, fielding their first serious mid-engined car in the late 1950s.

At first, established powers like Ferrari and Maserati viewed the Cooper concept as a curious sideshow. Yet at the 1958 Monaco Grand Prix, the tight and twisting circuit played into the nimble Cooper's hands. Stirling Moss's remarkable drive in a Rob Walker-entered Cooper, and subsequent successes by Jack Brabham and others, began turning skeptical heads. By 1959, Brabham's drivers' championship and Cooper's constructors' title using a rear-engined car conclusively demonstrated that the old front-engine formula was becoming obsolete.

This British breakthrough opened the door for a host of new names to assert themselves at motorsport's highest level. Vanwall—another British team—had already signaled that an all-British effort could outdo established continental marks when it beat Ferrari and Maserati to the Constructors' Championship in 1958. Now the stage was set for others. The British Racing Motors (BRM) team, originally conceived as a national project, overcame its early teething problems and began to challenge the Italian dominance. BRM scored significant successes in the early 1960s, culminating in Graham Hill's drivers' title in 1962 with the BRM P57.

Perhaps no individual better symbolized this era of British ascendancy than Colin Chapman, the engineering mastermind behind Team Lotus. Chapman was not just an engineer; he was an inventor, a visionary who refused to accept conventional wisdom. Embracing the rear-engine layout wholeheartedly, he believed a racing car could be continually refined, made lighter, and more aerodynamically efficient than any that had come before. His relentless pursuit of innovation led Lotus to develop the monocoque chassis—where the car's body itself formed a stressed structural shell—replacing traditional space-frame designs. Introduced in the 1962 Lotus 25, this concept reduced weight and increased rigidity, unlocking performance gains that would force every other constructor to follow suit.

With each passing season, the British influence deepened.

Suddenly, Italy's long-standing command of the front-engine era faced a formidable challenge. Lotus, Cooper, and BRM, soon joined by BRP (British Racing Partnership) and later McLaren, became consistent protagonists on the Grand Prix stage. Their workshops and test tracks were found in quiet corners of the English countryside, but the results of their engineering experiments were displayed to the world on circuits like Monza, Spa, and the Nürburgring. Racing had become a laboratory for British ingenuity, and every new success underscored the importance of innovation.

The rapid-fire pace of these changes distinguished this period from what came before. Traditionalists who once saw racing cars as simply "bigger engines, better drivers" learned that careful weight management, aerodynamics, and even the shape of the chassis could mean the difference between victory and defeat. Rear-engined cars were typically more compact, promoting better handling. Paired with Chapman's flair for radical design and the mechanical reliability that BRM and Coventry Climax engines soon offered, the British constructors commanded not just attention, but results.

Ultimately, the mid-engine revolution represented more than just a design alteration. It signaled the modern era of Grand Prix racing, one in which incremental engineering progress trumped old assumptions about how a car should be built and driven. This British ascendancy helped usher in a new professionalism: wind-tunnel testing, meticulous suspension geometry, and scientific approaches to fuel and tires became standard operating procedure. The cars, once brute-force machines, began to look and behave like agile, purposeful instruments of speed.

If the early 1950s had belonged to the might of Italian manufacturers and the artistry of drivers like Fangio and Ascari, the late 1950s and early 1960s belonged to the British innovators. With Cooper leading the way in proving that rear engines could win races, and Colin Chapman at Lotus refining that concept to perfection, a new chapter in Formula One history had begun. It was a chapter defined by radical thinking, technical adventure, and the undeniable shift of the balance of power northward, to the fertile engineering minds of Britain. This was the mid-engine revolution—and its effects would echo through motorsport for decades to come.

5. The New Wave of 1960s Driving Icons

As the 1960s rolled in, the face of international motorsport began to reflect a generation of drivers who were not only extraordinary in their chosen discipline, but who also willingly crossed the boundaries between racing series, continents, and car types. These new icons—figures like Jim Clark, Graham Hill, John Surtees, Dan Gurney, and Jack Brabham—did more than just win races. By taking on challenges in Formula One, the Indianapolis 500, endurance classics, and even sports car and touring car events, they helped redefine the very image of the racing driver. They were both specialists and generalists, showing that greatness behind the wheel could adapt to any format, any machine.

Jim Clark

Quiet and unassuming off the track, the Scottish farmer's son transformed into a maestro once he slipped behind the wheel. Jim Clark, driving predominantly for Lotus under Colin Chapman's guidance, seemed to move in concert with the car itself. His precision, smoothness, and almost uncanny ability to anticipate a machine's limits made him the ultimate driver's driver. Clark captured two Formula One World Championships (1963 and 1965) and, in one of his defining feats, crossed the Atlantic to conquer the Indianapolis 500 in 1965. His brilliance at Indy, a high-speed oval far removed from Europe's twisting circuits, showed that true driving talent could transcend geography and format. Clark's triumphs, achieved without fuss or bluster, radiated a quiet confidence that resonated with fans worldwide. Here was a driver who could switch from the Nürburgring's intimidating carousel to the Brickyard's four corners without missing a beat.

Graham Hill

In contrast to Clark's introverted persona, Graham Hill brought a natural showman's flair to racing. Debonair and witty, he was as recognizable in the paddock as on the circuit. Yet beneath this charm was a craftsman at the wheel. Hill earned two Formula One World Championships (1962 and 1968), and he would eventually become the only driver in history to claim motorsport's unofficial "Triple Crown" by winning the Monaco Grand Prix, the Indianapolis 500 (in 1966), and the 24 Hours of Le Mans (in 1972). During the 1960s, however, his star rose for his relentless pursuit of victory in F1 and his fearless ventures into the American single-seater scene. Hill's ability to adapt and excel across racing formats showcased the evolving nature of a global motorsport hero: charismatic, technically adept, and open to testing himself against the world's best on any stage.

John Surtees

If Hill's feats were impressive, John Surtees brought an entirely different dimension to motorsport versatility. Surtees first claimed fame as a multiple-time world champion on two wheels, dominating motorcycle Grand Prix racing with MV Agusta. When he switched to four wheels full-time in the 1960s, some doubted whether such a transition could produce results at the pinnacle of car racing. He proved them wrong, capturing the 1964 Formula One World Championship with Ferrari and thus becoming the only person ever to secure world titles in both motorcycle and automobile racing. His success demonstrated that fundamental skills—balance, timing, mechanical sensitivity—could be transferred between vastly different machines. Surtees's achievement stands as an enduring testament to adaptability and redefined what it meant to be a racing champion.

Dan Gurney

Meanwhile, American Dan Gurney embodied the international spirit of the sport. Racing as an expatriate in Formula One, he stood atop Grand Prix podiums for Porsche, Brabham, and his own Eagle team. Gurney's interests and successes reached beyond F1: he competed in the Indianapolis 500, NASCAR stock cars, and endurance events like the 24 Hours of Le Mans. His engineering mindset contributed to innovations, including the famous "Gurney flap" for aerodynamic efficiency. Gurney also broke cultural barriers. His victory celebrations, which included the first known instance of spraying champagne on a podium, reflected the growing sense of personality and entertainment value that drivers were bringing to the public. His approach, blending technical curiosity with a willingness to try everything, broadened the sport's horizons and showcased the versatility demanded of a true racing icon.

Jack Brabham

No discussion of this era's icons would be complete without Sir Jack Brabham. The Australian driver-engineer secured three Formula One championships (1959, 1960, 1966) and remains the only driver to win the title in a car bearing his own name. Brabham's mechanical aptitude and entrepreneurial spirit saw him guide the transition from front- to rear-engined layouts at Indianapolis, challenging the established American front-engined "roadsters" with his nimble, mid-engined Cooper in 1961. His pioneering efforts at Indy opened the door for the European influence in American racing. On top of this, Brabham's involvement in sports car racing and his collaboration with fellow innovators blurred the lines that previously separated continents and categories. Like the others, his success demonstrated that mastery on one circuit or in one formula was no longer the limit of what a top driver could achieve.

Shaping the Sport's Image

These men represented the new face of racing in the 1960s. Their achievements answered a question: could a single driver excel simultaneously in the tight, technical confines of European Grand Prix circuits, the full-throttle blasts of American ovals, and the grueling marathon that was endurance sports car racing? The answer, repeatedly, was yes. This versatility made them heroes not just to fans of one series or another, but to a broad, international audience. They appealed to enthusiasts who marveled at finesse, to newcomers who admired daring, and to casual observers struck by their global presence and personal style.

They shaped the image of the modern racing driver as a world traveler, a technologically savvy competitor as much at home on the wide expanses of an American superspeedway as the narrow streets of Monaco. Their successes, captured in newspapers, magazines, and, increasingly, in living-room television broadcasts, elevated the sport's profile. Motorsports, once considered a niche European pastime or a regional American entertainment, now looked like a grand global endeavor—populated by stars who could take on any challenge.

In the 1960s, these drivers became integral figures in the golden age narrative. They carried forward the tradition of skill and bravery embodied by Fangio and Ascari but applied it to a more interconnected world. By setting records on distant shores, crossing the Atlantic and Pacific in search of new opportunities, they reflected their time's spirit—an era defined by exploration, technological curiosity, and cultural exchange. In doing so, they helped motorsport grow beyond its earlier confines and established a standard of versatility and excellence that still resonates in the racing world today.

6. Formula One's Coming of Age

By the early 1950s, what had once been a collection of prestigious yet separate Grand Prix races began to coalesce into a truly global championship. The establishment of the Formula One World Championship in 1950 offered more than a title—it introduced structure, continuity, and a clear narrative that tied together drivers, teams, and manufacturers across an entire season. Over the next two decades, this framework would refine itself through evolving regulations and standards, shepherding the sport from a passionate pastime into a professional enterprise built on engineering prowess and meticulous preparation.

At the heart of this shift were the rules that defined what a Formula One car could and could not be. Initially, the FIA regulations were relatively broad, leaving ample room for large-displacement engines and substantial cars that bore a resemblance to pre-war machines. Yet as the decade moved on, the governing body's rule changes—such as the decision in 1954 to limit engine displacement to 2.5 liters—helped encourage more nuanced engineering. A different formula introduced in 1961 reduced maximum engine size to 1.5 liters, radically altering the design approach and fostering competition not just in raw power, but in efficiency, handling, and ingenuity.

Such rule shifts were not arbitrary. They reflected the FIA's attempts to balance speed, safety, cost, and the desire for close competition. Each regulatory step encouraged designers and constructors to think more deeply about how to optimize their cars within defined limits. Instead of just building bigger engines, teams had to explore lighter materials, more sophisticated suspensions, better brakes, and improved aerodynamics. The gradual proliferation of disc brakes, more precise steering systems, and the introduction of monocoque chassis design—popularized by Lotus—were direct responses to these evolving rules and the pressure to find every advantage possible.

These technical developments also went hand in hand with a growing professionalism among Grand Prix teams. Once, a handful of mechanics and an inspired team manager might suffice, and drivers might even roll up their sleeves to help tune their own engines. By the early 1960s, this model had begun to fade. Teams like Ferrari, BRM, and Lotus, as well as newcomers like McLaren, structured their organizations more like engineering outfits than gentlemanly clubs. Specialist roles emerged—engineers dedicated to chassis strength, aerodynamicists examining airflow, and mechanics who focused on rapid pit stops and efficient logistics. Testing became more rigorous, and the workshop transformed into a laboratory where innovation replaced intuition as the path to victory.

Powertrain innovation was at the heart of this evolution. As the formulas became more restrictive, engine builders looked beyond sheer displacement to extract greater horsepower and better torque curves from smaller units. Overhead camshafts, higher compression ratios, and more refined fuel mixtures came to define the top-performing engines. British teams often worked with Coventry Climax or BRM engines, while Ferrari developed its own powertrains.

Meanwhile, Honda and others would soon join the fray, lured by the challenge of engineering perfection and the allure of global prestige.

The relationship between team owners, drivers, and sponsors also matured. In earlier years, a charismatic driver might attract support almost single-handedly, and manufacturers raced primarily to showcase their marques. As the World Championship gained stature, companies began to see Formula One as a strategic marketing platform. This realization led to more stable budgets, better equipment, and a more reliable career path for drivers and team personnel. While major commercial sponsorship was still in its infancy, the seeds were being sown for an era where finance and corporate partnerships would become integral to the survival and success of any team.

All of these changes influenced how the sport was perceived by the public. In the 1950s, racing fans admired the bravery of drivers wrestling powerful but often temperamental machines. By the 1960s, spectators were beginning to appreciate the sport's technological nuance and sophistication. The narrative that once centered solely on daring pilots now encompassed brilliant engineers, methodical test drivers, and strategic minds operating behind the scenes. From the grandstands of Monza to the broadcast booths covering the British Grand Prix at Silverstone, observers recognized that the future of Formula One lay as much in the workshop and design studio as on the racing line.

The formalization of the championship and the constant fine-tuning of its regulations also made individual seasons more coherent stories to follow. Fans could track the ebb and flow of fortunes across multiple continents and circuits, witnessing how a rule change might benefit one team while challenging another. In this environment, motorsport evolved from a series of prestigious but loosely connected events into a structured, season-long battle of intellect, skill, and engineering creativity.

In essence, by the mid-1960s, Formula One had come of age. It no longer resembled the early days of post-war recovery, when each race felt like a standalone festival of speed. Instead, it had matured into a sophisticated and highly professional world championship—one that would set the standards and serve as the pinnacle for all forms of open-wheel racing. The golden age of motorsport was being defined not just by spectacle and star drivers, but by the underlying systems, standards, and ever-changing frontiers of technology that would guide the sport into its modern era.

7. Europe's Legendary Circuits and Classic Grands Prix

In the 1950s and 1960s, the heart of European motor racing beat strongest at a handful of circuits that had become as storied and celebrated as the drivers who conquered them. Each of these venues—be it the sweeping forests of the Nürburgring, the high-speed straights of Monza, the undulating curves of Spa-Francorchamps, or the narrow streets of Monaco—possessed a character so distinct that simply naming the track brought its challenges vividly to mind. To the fans who lined the barriers and the competitors who braved their dangers, these circuits were more than asphalt and Armco. They were shrines of speed, elemental tests of skill, and stages upon which modern motorsport's greatest dramas were enacted.

The Nürburgring (Germany)

Nestled in the Eifel Mountains of western Germany, the Nürburgring Nordschleife had earned a reputation by the 1950s as a course that demanded equal parts courage, discipline, and mechanical reliability. Its layout—over 14 miles in length, comprised of more than 170 corners—wound through dense forests and rose and fell with the natural contours of the land. For drivers, racing there was less about memorizing a handful of turns and more about committing an entire landscape to muscle memory. Jim Clark once admitted that he was never fully at ease on its treacherous tarmac, and Juan Manuel Fangio's 1957 victory at the Nürburgring, driving a Maserati and making up nearly a minute on the leading Ferraris, became one of the sport's enduring legends. The circuit's remote setting, unpredictable weather, and sheer complexity tested both man and machine to their very limits, elevating a good drive to an act of mastery and ensuring that a Nürburgring Grand Prix was always a landmark event in any championship campaign.

Monza (Italy)

If the Nürburgring was an intricate exam, Monza's Autodromo Nazionale was a speed cathedral. Located just outside Milan, Monza had hosted Grand Prix races since the 1920s, and its 1950s and '60s editions continued a legacy of breathtaking velocity. With long straights and wide curves, it dared drivers to hold the throttle open and seek the absolute top end of their cars' capabilities. Ferrari, Alfa Romeo, Maserati, and later BRM, Lotus, and others relished the chance to prove the performance and durability of their engines here. Monza's iconic banking, though gradually phased out of Formula One by the late 1960s, left a lasting image of cars hurtling around steeply inclined curves at speeds that defied logic. In Italy, racing was cultural bedrock, and Monza was its beating heart—a place where tifosi (the passionate Italian fans) roared approval from grandstands swathed in Ferrari red. Victories at Monza resonated beyond the realm of sport, touching on national pride and engineering prowess, giving the Italian Grand Prix a status that endures to this day.

Spa-Francorchamps (Belgium)

In Belgium's Ardennes countryside lay Spa-Francorchamps, a circuit that combined the best and worst of nature's elements. The original layout, an expansive 8.7-mile course using public roads, was famed for its dramatic elevation changes, sweeping high-speed corners, and the notorious unpredictability of its microclimate. Rain, fog, and even sunshine could appear in different sections of the track on the same lap, leaving drivers to wrestle with changing conditions at extraordinary speeds. Eau Rouge, a corner complex that soared uphill under heavy compression, became one of motor racing's most revered challenges. Spa rewarded bravery and punished recklessness: the courageous could find time by pushing through the mist at breakneck pace, yet a single miscalculation could end a race in a moment. For spectators and participants, Spa's grandeur was in its raw authenticity—a natural tapestry of roads that captured the essence of open-road racing traditions, even as the modern era grew more regulated and precise.

Monaco (Principality of Monaco)

While the Nürburgring, Monza, and Spa placed a premium on a car's power and a driver's nerve at high speeds, the Monaco Grand Prix offered something entirely different. Set against the glittering backdrop of the Mediterranean coastline, the tight, twisting streets of Monte Carlo became a circuit unlike any other. Armco barriers and stone walls stood mere inches from the racing line, leaving no room for error. The track was narrow, the surface bumpy, and the opportunity for overtaking minimal. Yet the challenges only added to Monaco's allure. To win here demanded absolute precision, technical finesse, and mental stamina. The glamour off the track—in the yachts lining the harbor, the celebrities in the grandstands, and the wealth of the principality—contrasted sharply with the harsh reality of the circuit. A Monaco win cemented a driver's status as a master of control and focus. It was, and remains, one of the crown jewels of the racing world.

Cultural and Historical Significance

These four circuits were not simply sports venues; they were woven into the cultural fabric of their respective regions. The Germans referred to the Nürburgring as "The Green Hell," a nickname coined by Jackie Stewart in a later era but rooted in the track's fearsome lore. The Italians adored Monza and the national heroes it showcased, making the track a place of annual pilgrimage for fans. Belgium's Spa evoked the romantic, if treacherous, era of motorsport that still bridged old-style road racing with modern Grand Prix competition. And Monaco's blend of opulence and difficulty made it a uniquely prestigious event, offering a stage where the world's finest drivers could prove their mettle against a circuit that demanded perfection.

By the 1960s, as regulations tightened and safety measures edged toward modernization, these circuits stood out as living links to racing's earlier days. They preserved the sport's raw authenticity, even as technology advanced and teams professionalized. To claim victory at any of these legendary venues was to etch one's name into motor racing history, often right alongside the greats who had previously tamed their asphalt ribbons.

For fans, the knowledge that these circuits demanded something special from the competitors heightened the drama of a Grand Prix weekend. Each track's personality was a talking point, shaping strategy and car setup, influencing driver confidence, and ultimately telling a richer story than could be found at more uniform, sanitized venues. The Europe of the 1950s and '60s offered these four iconic theaters where motorsport's golden age played out with all its noise, speed, and daring—a legacy that would endure, decades on, as an integral part of the sport's timeless mystique.

8. Sports Car Racing and Endurance Battles

Beyond the world of Grand Prix racing and closed-cockpit single-seaters, the 1950s and 1960s also saw the blossoming of a parallel narrative in sports car and endurance competition. These were battles fought not only on Europe's most storied circuits, but over roads and routes spanning entire regions. Fans who followed these endurance classics did so with a sense of awe, for here was motorsport at its most visceral: cars tested not merely in short sprints, but over hours, sometimes days, demanding a harmony of speed, durability, and meticulous strategy. At the forefront of this sphere stood the 24 Hours of Le Mans, the Mille Miglia, and the Targa Florio, each with its own distinctive character and place in motoring lore.

Le Mans: The Ultimate Test of Man and Machine

No endurance race carried as much global prestige as the 24 Hours of Le Mans. Held in France since 1923, Le Mans challenged entrants to survive a full rotation of the clock at near-top speeds, navigating the long Mulsanne Straight and the tricky bends of the Circuit de la Sarthe. By the 1950s, this event had evolved into a grand stage where manufacturers showcased their engineering prowess. Ferrari, Jaguar, Aston Martin, and later Porsche engaged in fierce rivalries, vying not just for victory, but for the credibility and marketing edge that a Le Mans win bestowed. Technological innovation thrived here: disc brakes, aerodynamic bodywork, and increasingly powerful engines evolved quickly under the relentless demands of a race where mechanical failures and driver fatigue were as much the enemy as rival teams. The sound of engines roaring through the French night, headlights carving through darkness and mist, became symbolic of a test both timeless and profound.

The Mille Miglia: Italy's Thousand-Mile Marathon

While Le Mans took place on a closed circuit, Italy's Mille Miglia covered roughly a thousand miles of public roads across towns, countryside, and mountain passes. Restored after the war, this open-road endurance trial captured the romantic essence of the sport's early spirit. Drivers of Ferraris, Maseratis, Porsches, and even smaller Italian marques raced from Brescia to Rome and back, cheered on by throngs of spectators who lined the roads—sometimes perilously close to the high-speed action. Here, strategy and mechanical sympathy mattered as much as raw pace. Alberto Ascari, Stirling Moss, and other greats set astonishing average speeds, defying the rough surfaces and unpredictable weather. Victories in the Mille Miglia elevated both driver and machine to folk-hero status, reinforcing the idea that a car's pedigree was forged not only on racetracks but on everyday roads transformed into a public theater of speed and daring.

The Targa Florio: Sicily's Demanding Mountain Course

The Targa Florio, held on the mountainous roads of Sicily, belonged to a similar tradition of endurance on public roads. Its narrow, twisting route through villages and along hillside curves tested handling, brakes, and driver concentration.

Here, a large and powerful engine counted for little if a car could not maneuver swiftly through tight corners and avoid countless hazards. The Targa Florio rewarded agility, resilience, and local knowledge. Stirling Moss once described it as one of the greatest challenges in racing, equating it not just to a test of machinery but to an athletic, even artistic endeavor. Victories on this island race carried a cultural weight—like Le Mans and the Mille Miglia, the Targa Florio was woven into local identity, making triumphs deeply meaningful for teams, drivers, and manufacturers looking to prove their mettle in a supremely demanding environment.

Rivalries and Technological Arms Races

The lure of these endurance contests attracted fierce competition among Europe's top manufacturers. Ferrari's blood-red cars emerged as consistent favorites, known for their powerful engines and chassis tuned through countless hours of testing. Jaguar's C-Types and D-Types, with their advanced disc brakes and aerodynamic finesse, challenged Ferrari's dominance at Le Mans. Aston Martin's DBR1 shocked many by winning in 1959, illustrating that a carefully developed underdog could topple mighty giants. Porsche, initially known for smaller, nimble cars, gradually honed its engineering to create machines capable of matching and then surpassing the titans in longer events, culminating in future decades of success at La Sarthe.

Advances came thick and fast. The development of aerodynamic bodywork and low-drag profiles allowed cars to maintain higher speeds safely. Engine reliability, once a weak link in endurance attempts, improved as carburetors gave way to fuel injection and as metallurgy and lubrication science advanced. Lightweight materials and more sophisticated suspension systems emerged as crucial performance factors, ensuring that the balance between power and efficiency became a defining theme of endurance racing's golden age.

Broadening Horizons and Global Prestige

Endurance racing's emphasis on manufacturer involvement meant that technical breakthroughs often had a direct impact on road cars, accelerating development cycles and lending prestige to successful brands. Jaguar's Le Mans triumphs, for instance, boosted the company's global reputation, while Ferrari's endurance pedigree added to the allure of owning one of its exotic road-going models. This interplay between track and road helped foster a vibrant marketplace of automotive innovation, feeding the public imagination and further intertwining racing success with brand image.

Culturally, events like Le Mans, the Mille Miglia, and the Targa Florio stood as tests of national character and ingenuity—France's historic endurance classic, Italy's beloved thousand-mile odyssey, and Sicily's grueling road battle each drew from deep wells of regional pride. Fans of the era followed these races in newspapers and magazines, eager to see whether British engineering could outsmart Italian flair, or whether a German marque like Porsche might finally dethrone an established champion. The prestige of these endurance events shaped the global motorsport landscape, reinforcing the idea that true greatness came from facing not just another competitor, but time, distance, and the very limits of human and mechanical endurance.

In that sense, sports car and endurance racing during the 1950s and '60s reflected the sport's broader golden age—an epoch defined not merely by how fast a car could lap a circuit, but by how gracefully it could dance through adversity, how reliably it could run hour after hour, and how effectively the synergy between driver and machine could ward off fatigue and failure. These endurance classics, legendary in their day and still revered decades later, captured a fundamental truth: that racing was as much about the journey's resilience as the speed at its destination.

9. The American Scene: Indy, USAC, and NASCAR

While European racing cemented its legendary circuits and endurance trials, the American motorsport landscape developed along its own distinct path during the 1950s and 1960s. The United States offered a different sort of racing culture—one that meshed with the nation's love of large, powerful automobiles, the spectacle of big events, and a rugged, no-nonsense ethos. At the heart of this culture stood the Indianapolis 500, a single event so prestigious that it shaped the direction of American open-wheel racing. Yet, the American racing story was larger than just Indy: USAC (the United States Auto Club) oversaw a series of ovals and road courses that produced homegrown heroes, while NASCAR, born from stock car roots, evolved into a national phenomenon under the guiding hand of Bill France Sr. Together, these forces would influence international racing culture, blurring the lines between what was considered "American" and "European" style competition.

Indianapolis 500: From Roadsters to Rear Engines

No American racing event commanded as much attention as the Indianapolis 500, held annually at the Indianapolis Motor Speedway in Indiana. In the early 1950s, the Speedway was home to front-engined "roadsters," heavy brutes that thundered around the 2.5-mile oval at astonishing speeds. Builders like A.J. Watson specialized in refining these beasts—low-slung machines with solid axles, Offenhauser engines, and a look and feel deeply rooted in American craftsmanship. Skilled drivers such as Bill Vukovich and

Rodger Ward tamed these cars, carving out legends in a uniquely American idiom.

But as the decade wore on, the influence of European engineering philosophies began to drift onto the American racing scene. In 1961, Jack Brabham brought a rear-engined Cooper to Indy, though it didn't immediately dethrone the roadsters. Still, his presence was a harbinger of change. By the mid-1960s, Lotus and other European-inspired builders introduced rear-engined cars that proved lighter, more nimble, and better balanced. The shift happened quickly: by the late 1960s, the front-engined roadster had all but disappeared from the Brickyard's starting grid, replaced by sleek, mid-engined machines. These cars drew on technologies and ideas from Formula One and sports car racing, signaling that the world's biggest single-day sporting event could not be isolated from global innovation. Indy had embraced a new era, one that would tie American open-wheel competition more closely to the international racing community.

The Role of USAC and Regional Heroes

This transformation did not stand alone. The USAC series—which sanctioned the Indianapolis 500 and other oval races—provided a ladder for American drivers to climb and prove themselves. Local short-track and dirt oval stars dreamed of making it to the Brickyard, forging a uniquely American driver development path. Racers like Parnelli Jones, Mario Andretti, and A.J. Foyt honed their craft on rough and tumble ovals before rising to Indy stardom. Their successes bridged the gap between grassroots racing and the pinnacle of American open-wheel competition, illustrating that mastery of local bullrings could translate into national fame and Indy glory.

While Europe had its richly historical road courses and Grand Prix disciplines, the United States revered oval racing's immediacy and accessibility. Racing in America felt close to the people: spectators in jeans and T-shirts packed bleachers alongside dusty tracks, cheering on the daring moves of drivers who might well have been their neighbors. The USAC universe was colorful and direct, suited to a nation that prized straight talk and unvarnished competition. By the 1960s, with Indy in full bloom and American drivers beginning to test their mettle internationally, the U.S. open-wheel scene had established a distinct identity while showing an openness to ideas from across the Atlantic.

NASCAR's Rise from the South to the Nation

Away from the polished grandeur of Indianapolis lay another narrative. Down in the American South, on dirt fairgrounds and rough local circuits, stock car racing had taken root before the war. By the late 1940s, Bill France Sr. had founded NASCAR (the National Association for Stock Car Auto Racing) to bring order and a points system to what had been a chaotic collection of loosely organized events. In the 1950s, NASCAR began to grow steadily, and as the 1960s dawned, it surged forward, fueled by a fan base that loved the rough-and-tumble spectacle of big, heavy cars banging fenders at high speed.

Unlike the specialized, purpose-built machines of Formula One or Indy, NASCAR's early contenders were cars that looked like what Americans drove on the streets—Ford, Chevrolet, Dodge, and Pontiac sedans and coupes, modified heavily for racing. This familiar aesthetic appealed to everyday fans, bridging the gap between the showroom and the speedway. Heroes like Lee Petty, Junior Johnson, and Fireball Roberts thrilled spectators with daring passes and fearless driving. By the mid-1960s, drivers like Richard Petty and David Pearson emerged as household names, their exploits followed in newspapers, on television broadcasts, and by fans who traveled long distances to attend races at Daytona, Darlington, and Talladega.

Under France's leadership, NASCAR sharpened its rules, improved its safety standards, and invested in promotion. As television coverage expanded, stock car racing spread beyond the South, capturing a national audience. The Daytona 500, founded in 1959, grew into NASCAR's flagship event—an American rival to the Indianapolis 500, built on banked turns and massive fields of cars racing in tight packs at speeds approaching 200 miles per hour. By the end of the 1960s, NASCAR had arrived as a major force in American culture, an empire of speed that welcomed sponsor involvement, broadcasting contracts, and celebrity drivers. It encapsulated American values—competition, accessibility, and a certain blue-collar grit—and presented them through the deafening spectacle of V8 engines and close-quarters racing.

A Distinct Yet Connected Culture

The 1950s and 1960s established America's motorsport identity as multifaceted, strongly regional at its core, yet internationally influenced. Indy's shift to rear-engined cars demonstrated that even traditions as entrenched as the front-engined roadster could yield to innovation from abroad. Meanwhile, NASCAR grew organically from a regional pastime into a nationwide attraction, forging a cultural institution that bore little resemblance to Europe's Grand Prix scene, yet was no less compelling to its devotees.

By the close of the 1960s, American racing was both its own vibrant ecosystem and a participant in the global motorsport conversation. Drivers like Dan Gurney and Mario Andretti proved that borders were porous, that an American could excel at Le Mans or in Formula One, and that European champions could find success at Indy. The American scene had thus carved out its unique place in the golden age of motorsport, complementing the elegance of European venues and the grandeur of endurance racing with a distinctive blend of spectacle, tradition, and a willingness to embrace change.

10. Cross-Pollination of Ideas: Europe Meets America

The 1950s and 1960s were not just periods of isolated innovation within European and American motorsport spheres; they were decades marked by a vibrant exchange of ideas, technologies, and philosophies between the Old and New Worlds. This cross-pollination fostered an environment where advancements in one region inspired breakthroughs in the other, leading to a richer, more dynamic global racing culture. Central to this narrative was the Ford GT40's triumph at Le Mans—a monumental achievement that epitomized the fusion of American ambition and European engineering prowess, forever altering the landscape of international motorsport.

Mutual Influences: Oval Innovations and European Adaptations

American oval racing, epitomized by events like the Indianapolis 500, was characterized by its emphasis on high-speed, straight-line performance and robust, powerful engines. These attributes led to innovations that eventually found their way into European racing circuits, which traditionally favored agility and handling over outright speed.

Aerodynamic Developments: One significant area of mutual influence was aerodynamics. American oval races demanded cars that could maintain stability at extreme speeds, pushing engineers to explore aerodynamic enhancements. Techniques such as streamlined bodywork and the incorporation of wings to provide downforce were honed on the high-speed ovals of America. European manufacturers, observing the effectiveness of these innovations, began integrating similar aerodynamic principles into their Grand Prix cars. This exchange accelerated the development of downforce techniques, which became essential for enhancing cornering speeds and overall vehicle stability in European circuits.

Engine and Powertrain Technologies: The powerful engines developed for American oval racing also influenced European manufacturers. The pursuit of higher horsepower and greater torque in engines led to advancements in fuel injection systems, turbocharging, and engine cooling technologies. European teams, recognizing the benefits of these robust powertrains, adapted and refined these technologies to suit the diverse demands of European Grand Prix circuits, where a balance of power and handling was crucial.

Chassis and Suspension Innovations: American racing's focus on durability and performance over long, sustained speeds prompted innovations in chassis design and suspension systems. Reinforced chassis and advanced suspension setups developed for endurance on oval tracks were adapted by European constructors to improve the handling and reliability of their racing cars on more technical circuits. This synergy resulted in more resilient and versatile vehicles capable of excelling in varied racing environments.

The Ford GT40: A Symbol of Transatlantic Collaboration

The Ford GT40 stands as a testament to the profound impact of cross-pollinated ideas between Europe and America. Born out of a fierce competition and driven by strategic collaboration, the GT40's success at Le Mans exemplified the power of combining American ambition with European engineering excellence.

Origins and Development: The story of the GT40 began in the early 1960s when Henry Ford II sought to challenge Ferrari's dominance at the 24 Hours of Le Mans. Ford's acquisition of Shelby American and the collaboration with British engineers laid the groundwork for a project that would blend American manufacturing capabilities with European design expertise. Under the leadership of engineers like Roy Lunn and team members from the British Motor Research Association, the GT40 was conceived as a high-performance, endurance racing machine capable of surpassing Ferrari's technological advancements.

Technological Synergy: The GT40 benefited from American innovation in engine design and manufacturing efficiency, while simultaneously incorporating European advancements in aerodynamics and chassis construction. The use of a lightweight, aluminum monocoque chassis—a concept refined by European constructors such as Lotus—combined with a powerful, high-revving Ford V8 engine, created a formidable package. This fusion of technologies addressed both the need for speed on the long straights of Le Mans and the agility required for handling the circuit's challenging corners.

Le Mans Triumphs: The culmination of this transatlantic collaboration was the GT40's performance at Le Mans. After initial setbacks and fierce competition, the GT40 finally achieved its breakthrough in 1966, when three of Ford's cars crossed the finish line in the top three positions—a historic sweep that shattered Ferrari's long-held dominance. This victory was not just a win for Ford but a symbolic moment that highlighted the successful integration of American and European racing philosophies and technologies.

Legacy and Influence: The GT40's triumph had lasting implications for international motorsport. It demonstrated that cross-continental collaboration could yield superior racing machines, inspiring future partnerships between American manufacturers and European engineering teams. The success of the GT40 also pushed other manufacturers to embrace a more global approach to racing development, fostering an environment where ideas and innovations flowed freely across borders.

Continued Exchange and Evolving Dynamics

The Ford GT40's success was a pivotal moment, but it was part of a broader, ongoing dialogue between Europe and America in motorsport. Throughout the 1960s, European manufacturers continued to adopt and adapt American innovations, while American teams and engineers integrated European technologies and design philosophies into their racing programs.

Shared Engineering Insights: Workshops and engineering teams from both continents frequently visited each other's factories and racing events, exchanging insights and best practices. This mutual learning environment accelerated the pace of technological advancement, ensuring that both European and American racing cars benefited from the latest developments in materials science, aerodynamics, and engine technology.

Driver Exchanges and Cultural Integration: Drivers also played a role in this cross-pollination. European drivers who competed in American races and vice versa brought back valuable experience and knowledge that influenced their home circuits. This cultural exchange enriched the racing community, fostering a more unified global motorsport culture where strategies and techniques were shared and refined collaboratively.

Impact on Modern Motorsport: The legacy of this transatlantic collaboration is evident in today's motorsport landscape. Modern Formula One and IndyCar vehicles incorporate technologies and design principles that have roots in both American and European innovations. The spirit of cooperation and shared progress that defined the GT40 era continues to drive the sport forward, ensuring that motorsport remains a global endeavor characterized by continuous innovation and mutual respect.

Conclusion: A Unified Motorsport World

The cross-pollination of ideas between Europe and America during the 1950s and 1960s was a defining feature of motorsport's golden age. Innovations developed on American ovals found new applications in European Grand Prix racing, while European engineering excellence inspired breakthroughs in American endurance and open-wheel racing. The Ford GT40's success at Le Mans encapsulated this harmonious blend of transatlantic collaboration, setting a precedent for future generations of racing technology and international cooperation.

This era demonstrated that the pursuit of speed and excellence transcended geographic boundaries, fostering a unified motorsport world where the best ideas, regardless of origin, could flourish. As we reflect on the golden age, it is clear that the mutual influences between Europe and America not only enriched the sport but also laid the groundwork for the sophisticated, globalized racing environment we witness today. The lessons learned and the innovations born from this cross-pollinated exchange continue to resonate, ensuring that the spirit of collaboration and relentless pursuit of improvement remains at the heart of motorsport's enduring legacy.

11. Mechanical Marvels: Engineering and Design Breakthroughs

The golden age of motorsport was not merely a spectacle of daring drivers and legendary races; it was a crucible of engineering innovation that transformed racing cars from brute-force machines into sophisticated, finely-tuned instruments of speed and agility. The 1950s and 1960s witnessed remarkable advancements in aerodynamics, materials science, braking systems, and suspension designs, all driven by the relentless pursuit of performance. Visionary engineers and pioneering constructors led these breakthroughs, forging the modern technologies that underpin today's racing machinery.

Advances in Aerodynamics

Aerodynamics emerged as a crucial factor in enhancing a car's performance, particularly as speeds increased and handling became paramount. Early racing cars primarily focused on minimizing air resistance, but the era saw a shift towards harnessing aerodynamic forces to improve grip and stability.

Streamlined Bodywork: The quest for reduced drag led to the development of more streamlined body shapes. Engineers experimented with various designs to achieve smoother airflow around the car, minimizing turbulence and drag. This period saw the transition from boxy, upright designs to more teardrop-shaped bodies that facilitated laminar airflow, allowing cars to slice through the air with greater efficiency.

Downforce and Wings: The introduction of aerodynamic wings revolutionized racing. Initially borrowed from aviation, wings were mounted on the cars to generate downforce, pressing the car firmly onto the track and enhancing tire grip during high-speed corners. The first noticeable implementation of wings was seen on cars like the Lotus 25, where the addition of a rear wing significantly improved stability and cornering speed.

Side Skirts and Air Dams: To further manipulate airflow, designers incorporated side skirts and air dams. Side skirts helped seal the sides of the car to prevent underbody airflow from disrupting the aerodynamic balance, while air dams directed air around the front wheels and under the car, reducing lift and increasing traction.

Materials: Spaceframe Chassis and Monocoques

The choice of materials and chassis design became pivotal in reducing weight while maintaining structural integrity. Two prominent innovations in chassis construction—spaceframe chassis and monocoque designs—transformed the engineering landscape.

Spaceframe Chassis: Spaceframe chassis utilized a framework of interconnected tubular steel or aluminum members, forming a lightweight yet rigid structure. This design allowed engineers to distribute stress more evenly throughout the chassis, enhancing the car's handling and durability. Constructors like Cooper and BRM employed spaceframe designs to achieve a balance between strength and weight, contributing to the mid-engine revolution's success.

Monocoque Construction: Colin Chapman of Lotus was a leading proponent of monocoque chassis construction, where the car's body itself served as the primary structural element. Introduced with the Lotus 25 in 1962, the monocoque design replaced the traditional spaceframe with a single-shell construction made from lightweight materials such as aluminum and later, carbon fiber composites. This approach significantly reduced weight and increased rigidity, allowing for greater performance and safety. The monocoque chassis became a standard in Formula One, setting the stage for future advancements in racing car design.

Disc Brakes: Enhanced Stopping Power

The transition from drum brakes to disc brakes marked a significant improvement in braking performance and reliability. Disc brakes offered superior heat dissipation, reducing brake fade during intense racing conditions and providing more consistent stopping power.

Introduction and Adoption: Jaguar was one of the first manufacturers to adopt disc brakes in motorsport, equipping their C-Type and D-Type cars with these advanced systems. The 1953 Le Mans victory of the Jaguar C-Type, powered by disc brakes, showcased their effectiveness in high-speed endurance racing. Disc brakes quickly gained popularity among constructors, including Ferrari, Maserati, and later, Lotus, as they recognized the performance benefits of improved braking efficiency.

Technological Refinements: Throughout the 1950s and 1960s, engineers continued to refine disc brake technology, enhancing materials and designs to withstand the rigors of racing. The use of ventilated discs, high-temperature resistant brake pads, and more precise caliper mechanisms contributed to the overall advancement of braking systems, making them an integral component of modern racing cars.

Suspension Systems: Precision and Adaptability

Advanced suspension systems played a crucial role in improving a car's handling and ride quality, allowing drivers to maintain better control during high-speed maneuvers and uneven track surfaces.

Independent Suspension: The move towards independent suspension systems allowed each wheel to move independently, providing better traction and stability. This was a departure from the rigid axle setups of earlier racing cars, which limited handling capabilities. Independent suspension enabled smoother cornering and more precise control, enhancing overall performance.

Double Wishbone and Coil Springs: Engineers experimented with different suspension geometries, such as the double wishbone setup, which provided superior camber control and minimized tire wear. Coupled with coil springs, these designs allowed for better shock absorption and more responsive handling. Lotus, under Colin Chapman's leadership, was at the forefront of implementing these sophisticated suspension systems, contributing to the superior performance of their racing cars.

Adjustable Dampers: Adjustable dampers became a staple in racing cars, allowing teams to fine-tune the suspension settings based on track conditions and driver preferences. This adaptability was crucial for optimizing performance across different circuits, whether they demanded tight handling or high-speed stability.

Mid-Century Engineering Visionaries

The transformative advancements in racing car engineering were driven by a cadre of visionary engineers and constructors who dared to push the boundaries of what was possible.

Colin Chapman (Lotus): Colin Chapman was a relentless innovator whose contributions to racing car design were revolutionary. His emphasis on lightweight construction, advanced aerodynamics, and the monocoque chassis fundamentally changed the Formula One landscape. Chapman's philosophy of "adding lightness" not only improved performance but also influenced broader automotive engineering practices.

Enzo Ferrari (Ferrari): Enzo Ferrari's passion for racing and his relentless pursuit of perfection propelled Ferrari to the forefront of motorsport. Under his leadership, Ferrari developed powerful, reliable engines and embraced new technologies such as disc brakes and aerodynamic bodywork. Ferrari's success in both Formula One and endurance racing underscored the importance of combining engineering excellence with competitive spirit.

Bruce McLaren (McLaren): Bruce McLaren, a driver-turned-engineer, founded McLaren Racing with a focus on innovation and precision engineering. His designs featured advanced aerodynamics and lightweight materials, setting new standards in Formula One. McLaren's commitment to technological advancement and team professionalism contributed significantly to the evolution of modern racing technology.

Carlo Chiti (Ferrari and Tec-Mec): Carlo Chiti was a key figure in Ferrari's engineering team before founding his own Tec-Mec company. Chiti was instrumental in developing some of Ferrari's most successful engines and chassis during the 1950s and 1960s. His expertise in engine tuning and chassis dynamics played a crucial role in Ferrari's dominance in both Formula One and endurance racing.

John Cooper (Cooper Car Company): John Cooper's pioneering work with the Cooper Car Company was central to the mid-engine revolution. Cooper's designs emphasized lightweight construction and balanced weight distribution, which proved to be highly effective in Grand Prix racing. His innovations not only transformed his own team's fortunes but also influenced the broader racing community to adopt similar mid-engine layouts.

Forging Modern Racing Technology

The technological breakthroughs of the 1950s and 1960s laid the groundwork for the sophisticated racing machines we see today. The era was characterized by a symbiotic relationship between driver skill and engineering innovation, where each advancement propelled the other forward.

Integration of Electronics: While still in its infancy, the integration of electronic components began to take shape during this period. Early forms of telemetry and data acquisition systems allowed teams to monitor engine performance and car behavior in real-time, providing valuable insights for further refinement.

Material Science Advances: The exploration of new materials, such as aluminum alloys and early composites, reduced weight while maintaining strength and durability. These advancements not only enhanced performance on the track but also influenced road car design, bridging the gap between racing technology and everyday automotive applications.

Computational Design: The seeds of computational design and simulation were planted as engineers sought to optimize aerodynamics and chassis performance. Wind tunnels became essential tools for testing and refining aerodynamic profiles, enabling more precise and effective designs based on empirical data.

Safety Innovations: As speeds increased, so did the focus on safety. Innovations such as fire-resistant driver suits, improved helmet designs, and the introduction of roll bars and cockpit protection systems were critical developments. These advancements reflected a growing awareness of the inherent dangers of motorsport and the need to protect drivers without compromising performance.

Conclusion: The Legacy of Engineering Excellence

The 1950s and 1960s were a testament to the ingenuity and

creativity of racing engineers who transformed motorsport into a high-tech arena of innovation. The advancements in aerodynamics, materials, braking systems, and suspension designs not only elevated the performance and safety of racing cars but also set the stage for the technological evolution of the sport. Visionaries like Colin Chapman, Enzo Ferrari, Bruce McLaren, Carlo Chiti, and John Cooper pushed the boundaries of engineering, forging the modern racing technologies that continue to shape motorsport today.

Their legacy is evident in every aspect of contemporary racing, from the sleek aerodynamics of modern Formula One cars to the lightweight, rigid chassis that ensure both speed and safety. The mechanical marvels of the mid-century era were not merely incremental improvements; they were revolutionary changes that redefined what was possible on the racetrack. As motorsport continued to evolve, the innovations of the 1950s and 1960s remained foundational, inspiring future generations of engineers and drivers to pursue excellence with the same relentless passion that defined the golden age of speed.

12. Safety on the Edge: Dangers and Disasters

The golden age of motorsport, characterized by exhilarating speeds and groundbreaking engineering, was also a period marked by significant peril. The 1950s and 1960s witnessed numerous tragedies that underscored the inherent dangers of racing. These fatal accidents, often involving top drivers and occurring during prestigious events, exposed the vulnerabilities of the sport and catalyzed a growing awareness of the need for enhanced safety measures. While racing during this era was imbued with glamour and heroism, it was equally shadowed by the ever-present threat of disaster, prompting the first cautious steps toward making the sport safer for its participants.

Fatalities of Top Drivers and the 1955 Le Mans Catastrophe

Motorsport in the mid-20th century was fraught with risk, and the loss of life was tragically common. The 1955 24 Hours of Le Mans remains one of the darkest chapters in racing history, emblematic of the era's perilous nature. On June 11, 1955, a catastrophic crash claimed the lives of 83 spectators and driver Pierre Levegh, making it the deadliest accident in motorsport history. Levegh's Mercedes-Benz W196 collided with a steel fence after a series of chain-reaction crashes, sending debris flying into the stands. The sheer scale of the disaster highlighted the insufficient safety measures in place, including inadequate barriers and the proximity of spectators to the track.

This tragedy was not an isolated incident. The 1950s saw the deaths of several prominent drivers, including Alberto

Ascari in a testing accident in 1955 and Stirling Moss at Goodwood in 1962, though Moss survived serious injuries. The loss of Juan Manuel Fangio's teammate, Luigi Musso, during practice for the 1958 Monaco Grand Prix further underscored the high stakes of the sport. Each fatality sent shockwaves through the racing community, prompting debates about the balance between speed, competition, and safety.

Numerous Near-Fatal Crashes

Beyond the fatalities, countless near-miss incidents highlighted the constant danger drivers faced. The Nürburgring Nordschleife, with its 14-mile length and over 170 corners, was a particular hotspot for accidents. Drivers like Jim Clark and Peter Collins survived harrowing crashes that left them with severe injuries, serving as grim reminders of the fine line between triumph and tragedy. The 1967 Italian Grand Prix at Monza saw Peter Revson crash into the barriers at high speed, escaping with only minor injuries, but the event reinforced the inherent risks of high-speed racing.

These near-fatal crashes were not limited to open-wheel racing. Endurance events like the Targa Florio and the Mille Miglia, which took place on public roads, also saw their share of deadly accidents. The combination of high speeds, challenging terrain, and less-than-ideal safety infrastructures made these races particularly perilous. Each incident fueled the growing consensus that significant changes were necessary to protect drivers and spectators alike.

Growing Awareness and the First Hesitant Steps Toward Improvement

The mounting casualties and near-disasters of the 1950s and 1960s gradually shifted the racing community's perspective on safety. While the sport had long been associated with bravery and risk, the losses began to challenge the status quo, fostering a nascent movement toward enhanced safety protocols. These initial steps were cautious and often met with resistance, as tradition and the pursuit of speed frequently overshadowed safety considerations.

Improved Circuit Designs: One of the first areas to see safety improvements was circuit design. Following the Le Mans disaster, significant changes were made to prevent similar tragedies. Tracks began to implement better barriers, increased runoff areas, and improved spectator stands to reduce the risk of debris reaching the crowd. The Nürburgring, for example, underwent modifications to enhance safety, including the addition of guardrails and the separation of spectator areas from the racing line.

Fire-Resistant Suits and Helmets: Driver safety equipment saw gradual enhancements as well. Fire-resistant suits became more common, offering better protection against flames in the event of a crash. Helmets evolved from simple leather caps to more robust designs incorporating advanced materials like fiberglass and, later, composites. These helmets provided better head protection, reducing the severity of injuries sustained during impacts.

Safer Cockpit Structures: Innovations in cockpit design also played a crucial role in improving driver safety. The introduction of roll bars and later monocoque chassis designs significantly enhanced structural integrity, protecting drivers in the event of a rollover or frontal collision. Teams began to prioritize the development of enclosed cockpits, which offered additional protection against debris and impacts.

Regulatory Changes and Safety Standards: The Fédération Internationale de l'Automobile (FIA) began to implement stricter safety regulations, although these changes were often slow to take hold. Rules regarding car construction, circuit safety, and driver equipment were gradually tightened to address the evolving understanding of racing dangers. For instance, the mandatory use of seat belts and the banning of certain hazardous car features reflected a shift towards prioritizing driver well-being over pure performance.

Emergence of Safety Advocates: Visionary figures within the racing community began to advocate for safety improvements. Drivers like Jackie Stewart became outspoken proponents of enhanced safety measures, pushing for better circuit designs, improved medical facilities, and stricter regulations. Stewart's efforts, among others, laid the groundwork for the comprehensive safety initiatives that would later transform the sport.

The Road to Modern Safety Standards

These early, hesitant steps towards safety were just the beginning. The experiences of the 1950s and 1960s set the stage for more profound and systematic safety reforms in subsequent decades. While the immediate changes were modest, they represented a crucial shift in mindset—from accepting danger as an inherent part of racing to actively seeking ways to mitigate it.

The legacy of this era's tragedies and near-misses is a testament to the resilience and adaptability of the motorsport community. Each loss and close call served as a catalyst for reflection and improvement, ensuring that the lessons learned would inform the future of racing. The gradual enhancements in circuit safety, driver protection, and regulatory oversight laid the foundation for the sophisticated safety systems that define modern motorsport.

Conclusion: A Dual Legacy of Speed and Caution

The 1950s and 1960s were a time of both remarkable achievement and profound loss in motorsport. The fatalities and disasters of this period highlighted the urgent need for improved safety measures, driving the first cautious steps toward making racing safer. These early efforts, though modest, were essential in shifting the culture of motorsport to prioritize the well-being of its participants alongside the pursuit of speed and victory.

As the golden age progressed, the lessons learned from these tragedies would lead to more comprehensive safety innovations, transforming the sport into a safer, more regulated endeavor. The dual legacy of this era—its breathtaking advancements and its heartbreaking losses—remains a pivotal chapter in the history of motorsport, reminding us that the pursuit of speed must always be balanced with the imperative of safety.

13. Rivalries and National Pride

The golden age of motorsport was as much a battleground of national pride and industrial prowess as it was a contest of speed and skill. The 1950s and 1960s saw intense rivalries among manufacturers and nations, each striving to assert their dominance on the global racing stage. Central to these rivalries were iconic names like Mercedes-Benz, Ferrari, and British constructors such as Lotus and BRM. These competitions were deeply intertwined with the broader geopolitical climate of the Cold War, where economic strength and technological innovation were seen as extensions of national prestige and ideological superiority.

Mercedes-Benz's Early Dominance and Eventual Withdrawal

Mercedes-Benz entered the 1950s Grand Prix scene with a formidable presence. The German manufacturer had already established a legacy of engineering excellence and technical innovation. In 1954, Mercedes-Benz made a triumphant return to Formula One with the W196, a car that combined advanced aerodynamics, fuel-injected engines, and lightweight construction. Drivers such as Juan Manuel Fangio and Stirling Moss brought Mercedes-Benz to the forefront, securing multiple victories and championships.

Dominance on the Track: Mercedes-Benz's W196 was a marvel of engineering, featuring a streamlined monocoque chassis and a fuel-injected straight-eight engine that produced unprecedented power and reliability. The car's aerodynamic efficiency allowed it to dominate circuits like Monza and Spa-Francorchamps, where high speeds and technical prowess were essential for success. Fangio's skillful driving complemented the car's capabilities, leading Mercedes-Benz to secure the Constructors' Championship in 1954 and 1955.

The 1955 Le Mans Catastrophe and Withdrawal: However, Mercedes-Benz's racing dominance was abruptly halted by the tragic events of the 1955 24 Hours of Le Mans. A catastrophic crash involving the Mercedes-Benz W196 driven by Pierre Levegh resulted in the deaths of Levegh and 82 spectators, making it the deadliest accident in motorsport history. The disaster had a profound impact on Mercedes-Benz and the entire racing community. In the aftermath, Mercedes-Benz withdrew from motorsport, citing concerns over safety and the inherent dangers of high-speed racing. This withdrawal created a vacuum in the racing world, paving the way for other manufacturers to seize the opportunity to dominate the sport.

Ferrari's Enduring Mystique

Amidst Mercedes-Benz's exit, Ferrari continued to build its enduring mystique, becoming synonymous with passion, performance, and Italian excellence. Under the leadership of Enzo Ferrari, the Scuderia Ferrari team became the heart and soul of Italian motorsport, embodying the nation's fervent love for racing and automotive engineering.

Legacy of Enzo Ferrari: Enzo Ferrari's vision was not merely to win races but to create a legacy of excellence and innovation. Ferrari's cars were celebrated for their distinctive design, powerful engines, and relentless performance. Drivers like Alberto Ascari, who secured consecutive World Championships in 1952 and 1953, and later, Phil Hill and John Surtees, became emblematic of Ferrari's competitive spirit and technical superiority.

Iconic Models and Innovations: Ferrari introduced several iconic models during this period, such as the Ferrari 500 TR and the Ferrari 625. These cars featured advanced engineering solutions, including the use of spaceframe chassis and sophisticated suspension systems, which provided superior handling and reliability. Ferrari's commitment to innovation ensured that their cars remained at the cutting edge of motorsport technology, maintaining their position as a dominant force in Formula One and endurance racing.

Rivalries and Championships: Ferrari's rivalry with emerging British teams like Lotus and BRM added a new dimension to the sport. Battles on the track were not just between drivers but between nations and their respective engineering philosophies. Ferrari's success in both Formula One and endurance races like Le Mans reinforced Italy's reputation as a powerhouse in motorsport, driven by a blend of passion and technical expertise.

Britain's Fervent Engineering Push

While Italy solidified its dominance through Ferrari, Britain emerged as a new epicenter of motorsport innovation, driven by a fervent engineering push from constructors like Lotus, BRM, Cooper, and later, McLaren. British teams brought fresh ideas and technological advancements that challenged the established order, ushering in a new era of competitiveness and ingenuity.

The Rise of British Constructors: British constructors were instrumental in revolutionizing Formula One racing. Teams like Cooper pioneered the mid-engine layout, which offered better weight distribution and handling compared to the traditional front-engine designs favored by manufacturers like Ferrari. This innovation quickly proved its merit, with Cooper drivers winning the World Championship in 1959 and 1960, signaling a shift in the competitive landscape.

Lotus and Colin Chapman: Colin Chapman, the founder of Lotus, was a key figure in British motorsport engineering. Chapman's philosophy of "adding lightness" emphasized reducing weight to enhance performance, leading to the development of lightweight chassis and aerodynamic designs. The introduction of the Lotus 25 in 1962, featuring a monocoque chassis, set new standards for structural integrity and performance. Chapman's relentless pursuit of innovation and his ability to adapt to changing regulations kept Lotus at the forefront of Formula One, earning multiple championships and influencing the broader engineering community.

BRM and British Racing Motors: British Racing Motors (BRM), another prominent British constructor, aimed to create a national team that could compete with the best in the world. Despite early struggles, BRM achieved success with models like the BRM P57, which won the 1962 World Championship with Graham Hill. BRM's focus on developing powerful, reliable engines and advanced aerodynamics contributed to Britain's reputation as a hub of racing innovation.

Cooper's Mid-Engine Revolution: John Cooper and the Cooper Car Company played a pivotal role in the mid-engine revolution. Cooper's designs emphasized balanced weight distribution and superior handling, which proved advantageous on the increasingly technical Formula One circuits. The success of Cooper's mid-engine cars not only earned championships but also inspired other British teams to adopt similar layouts, fundamentally altering the design philosophy of racing cars.

The Interplay of Cold War-Era Economics, National Pride, and Industry Competition

The Cold War era was a time of intense geopolitical rivalry, with nations vying for technological and economic superiority. This global context had a significant impact on motorsport, where racing was not just a sport but also a platform for demonstrating national prowess and industrial capabilities.

National Pride and Motorsport: Motorsport became a stage where national pride was on display. Success in racing was seen as a reflection of a country's engineering excellence and industrial strength. For Italy, Ferrari's victories were a testament to Italian craftsmanship and design ingenuity. Similarly, Britain's rise in motorsport was a source of national pride, showcasing the country's engineering talent and innovative spirit.

Economic Factors and Industrial Competition: The economic conditions of the Cold War era influenced motorsport in several ways. European manufacturers like Ferrari and British teams invested heavily in racing as a means of promoting their brands and demonstrating their technological advancements. The competition between these manufacturers was not just about winning races but also about outpacing rivals in engineering and innovation.

Technological Innovation as a Symbol of Superiority: Technological advancements in motorsport were closely linked to broader industrial competition. Innovations in aerodynamics, engine performance, and chassis design were seen as indicators of a country's technological edge. The relentless pursuit of speed and efficiency in racing cars mirrored the technological race between the superpowers, where breakthroughs in one field often had ripple effects across others.

Influence of Political and Economic Policies: Government policies and economic strategies also played a role in shaping motorsport. In countries like Italy and Britain, the support of national industries and manufacturers was crucial for the development and success of racing teams. This support often translated into state-backed research and development initiatives that fueled motorsport innovation.

Globalization of Motorsport: The interplay of Cold War dynamics contributed to the globalization of motorsport. European and American teams and manufacturers began to exchange ideas and technologies, breaking down previous barriers and fostering a more interconnected racing world. This exchange was exemplified by events like the Ford GT40's success at Le Mans, which symbolized the fusion of American ambition and European engineering excellence.

Conclusion: A Battleground of Nations and Innovation

The rivalries of the 1950s and 1960s were more than just competitions between teams and drivers; they were manifestations of national pride and industrial ambition. Mercedes-Benz's early dominance and subsequent withdrawal, Ferrari's enduring mystique, and Britain's fervent engineering push created a dynamic and competitive environment that propelled motorsport into a new era of innovation and global significance.

The Cold War-era interplay of economics, national pride, and industry competition infused motorsport with an added layer of intensity and purpose. Racing became a venue where nations could showcase their technological prowess and strategic ingenuity, turning each Grand Prix into a symbolic contest of national superiority. This period laid the foundation for the modern motorsport landscape, where the legacy of these rivalries and the spirit of national pride continue to influence the sport's evolution.

As we move forward in this exploration of motorsport's golden age, the enduring impact of these rivalries and the drive for national and industrial excellence will remain a central theme, illustrating how the pursuit of speed and victory transcended the boundaries of the racetrack to become a reflection of the broader societal and geopolitical currents of the time.

14. Commercialization and the Start of Sponsorship

The 1950s and 1960s marked a transformative period in motorsport, not only in terms of technological advancements and driver prowess but also in the way the sport was financed, marketed, and consumed by the public. This era witnessed the gradual shift from purely manufacturer-backed racing efforts to the emergence of commercial sponsorship, fundamentally altering the business landscape of motorsport. The introduction of branding on cars, evolving business models, and the burgeoning influence of television coverage redefined how teams operated and how the sport engaged with a global audience.

Shifting from Manufacturer-Backed Efforts to Commercial Sponsorship

In the early days of motorsport, racing teams were predominantly funded by the manufacturers themselves. Companies like Ferrari, Mercedes-Benz, and Alfa Romeo invested heavily in their racing programs as a means to showcase their engineering prowess and enhance their brand prestige. These manufacturer-backed teams operated with significant resources, focusing on technological innovation and competitive success to drive sales and reputation.

However, as the sport grew in popularity and complexity, the financial demands of competing at the highest levels began to exceed what manufacturers alone could sustain. The increasing costs of research and development, logistics, and driver salaries necessitated new funding sources. This financial pressure paved the way for the introduction of commercial sponsorship, marking a pivotal shift in the economic structure of motorsport.

Early Sponsorship Deals: The late 1950s and early 1960s saw the first instances of commercial sponsorship in racing. These early sponsors were often local businesses seeking to gain visibility through association with popular racing teams and events. One notable example was Shell Oil, which became involved with Team Lotus in the early 1960s. Shell's sponsorship provided essential financial support that allowed Lotus to develop more competitive cars, thereby enhancing the brand's visibility and prestige both on and off the track.

Another early sponsor was Marlboro, which began its long-standing relationship with racing teams by sponsoring drivers and events. Marlboro's involvement in motorsport not only provided financial backing but also introduced the concept of branded liveries, where sponsors' logos and colors became prominent features on racing cars.

Branding on Cars: The Birth of the Livery

The advent of commercial sponsorship brought about a significant change in the visual identity of racing cars. Branding on cars, known as liveries, became a crucial aspect of team identity and marketing strategy. This practice allowed sponsors to advertise their brands directly to spectators and television audiences, transforming racing cars into moving billboards.

Iconic Liveries: One of the most iconic examples of early car liveries is the red of Ferrari, which became synonymous with speed, passion, and Italian excellence. However, with the rise of commercial sponsors, teams began to experiment with more diverse and colorful liveries. Team Lotus, under Colin Chapman, adopted a striking blue and yellow livery when sponsored by Gold Leaf tobacco company. This vibrant color scheme not only made the cars more visually appealing but also significantly increased brand recognition for Gold Leaf.

Impact on Team Identity: Branding through liveries also influenced team dynamics and marketing approaches. Teams began to tailor their designs to align with sponsors' branding requirements, creating a symbiotic relationship where both the team and the sponsor benefited. This alignment helped teams secure more substantial financial backing, enabling further technological advancements and competitive success.

Changing Business Models: From Passion Projects to Professional Enterprises

The introduction of commercial sponsorship necessitated a shift in how racing teams operated. No longer were they solely passion projects driven by manufacturer interest and driver enthusiasm; they became professional enterprises with business strategies and financial planning at their core.

Revenue Diversification: Teams began to diversify their revenue streams beyond manufacturer support. Sponsorship deals, merchandising, and media rights became essential components of a team's income. This diversification allowed teams to sustain higher levels of competition, invest in research and development, and expand their operations globally.

Professional Management: The increasing commercialization also led to the professionalization of team management. Teams started employing specialized roles such as marketing managers, sponsorship coordinators, and financial analysts to handle the complexities of commercial partnerships and financial management. This professional approach ensured that teams could maximize the benefits of their sponsorship deals and maintain financial stability.

Case Study: Ferrari and Shell Partnership: Ferrari's partnership with Shell is a prime example of the evolving business model in motorsport. Shell's sponsorship provided Ferrari with the necessary funds to invest in cutting-edge technology and top-tier drivers. In return, Shell gained prominent brand visibility through Ferrari's success on the track. This mutually beneficial relationship exemplified how commercial sponsorship could enhance both team performance and sponsor marketing objectives.

The Influence of Emerging Television Coverage

Television emerged as a game-changer for motorsport in the 1950s and 1960s, expanding the sport's reach from local audiences to a global viewership. The visual medium of television amplified the impact of commercial sponsorship and branding, transforming racing into a widely consumed spectacle.

Broadcast Innovations: Early television broadcasts of motorsport events brought the thrill of racing into homes around the world. Networks began to recognize the potential of motorsport as a lucrative broadcasting commodity, leading to increased investment in race coverage and production quality. The ability to broadcast live races meant that sponsors could achieve unparalleled exposure, further incentivizing their involvement.

Sponsorship Value: Television coverage significantly enhanced the value of sponsorship deals. Brands realized that a successful race could lead to substantial brand recognition through repeated exposure during broadcasts. This realization led to more lucrative and long-term sponsorship agreements, as sponsors sought to capitalize on the extensive reach of television.

Global Fanbase: The global dissemination of race broadcasts helped build an international fanbase, transcending geographical boundaries and cultural differences. Sponsors could now market their brands to a broader audience, increasing their return on investment and solidifying their presence in the global market.

Technological Integration: Television also influenced the technological integration within racing teams. Teams began to consider the visual appeal of their cars and liveries, knowing that their cars would be scrutinized by millions of viewers. This led to more attention to aesthetics and branding, alongside performance and engineering excellence.

Key Milestones in Commercialization and Sponsorship

Several key milestones in the 1950s and 1960s illustrate the growing importance of commercialization and sponsorship in motorsport:

1961 Formula One Season: The 1961 Formula One season saw the first major sponsor liveries with the introduction of Gold Leaf on Team Lotus. This marked a significant shift from traditional manufacturer colors to branded liveries, setting a precedent for future sponsorship deals.

Ford GT40 and Corporate Sponsorship: The Ford GT40 project was heavily supported by corporate sponsorship, including backing from significant brands like Ford itself. The success of the GT40 at Le Mans in the mid-1960s underscored the potential of corporate-sponsored racing programs to achieve both competitive success and brand promotion.

Rise of Corporate Giants: Throughout the 1960s, corporate giants such as Shell, Marlboro, and Gulf Oil became increasingly prominent sponsors in motorsport. Their substantial investments enabled teams to push the boundaries of engineering and performance, while also benefiting from the extensive brand exposure racing provided.

Impact on the Sport's Evolution

The commercialization and emergence of sponsorship fundamentally altered the trajectory of motorsport, influencing everything from team structures and car designs to the global reach and financial sustainability of the sport.

Enhanced Competition: With increased funding from sponsors, teams could afford better technology, hire top-tier drivers, and conduct more extensive research and development. This led to a higher level of competition, as well-funded teams were better equipped to develop innovative solutions and gain a competitive edge.

Global Expansion: Commercial sponsorship facilitated the global expansion of motorsport. Teams with substantial financial backing could travel to international circuits, participate in a wider range of events, and build a global presence. This globalization helped transform motorsport into a truly international sport, attracting fans and sponsors from around the world.

Legacy of Sponsorship: The foundations laid in the 1950s and 1960s for commercial sponsorship have had a lasting legacy on motorsport. Today, sponsorship remains a critical component of racing, with multi-million-dollar deals and global brand partnerships being commonplace. The early adoption of sponsorship principles set the stage for the sophisticated marketing and financial strategies that define modern motorsport.

Conclusion: The Dawn of a Commercial Era

The 1950s and 1960s were pivotal in shaping the commercial landscape of motorsport. The transition from manufacturer-only funding to the inclusion of commercial sponsorship marked the beginning of a new era where financial support and brand partnerships became integral to team success and the sport's growth. The advent of branded liveries, evolving business models, and the influence of television coverage not only enhanced the sport's appeal and accessibility but also laid the groundwork for the highly commercialized and globally recognized motorsport industry we see today.

As motorsport continued to evolve, the principles and practices established during this golden age of commercialization would prove essential in sustaining the sport's popularity and competitiveness. The integration of commercial interests with racing excellence created a symbiotic relationship that propelled motorsport into a new dimension, where the pursuit of speed and the pursuit of brand success went hand in hand, shaping the future of racing for generations to come.

15. Media, Glamour, and Celebrity Culture

The golden age of motorsport was not only a period of intense competition and technological innovation but also an era where the sport intertwined with broader cultural trends, particularly in media and celebrity culture. The 1950s and 1960s saw motorsport transition from a niche passion to a mainstream spectacle, driven by the proliferation of media coverage and the emergence of racing drivers as glamorous, jet-setting celebrities. This chapter explores how magazines, newsreels, and the advent of televised racing expanded the sport's audience, and how drivers became icons of style and sophistication, shaping the public's perception of motorsport.

Magazines, Newsreels, and the Birth of Televised Racing

Before the age of television, motorsport's reach was primarily limited to those who could attend races in person or follow them through print media and newsreels. However, the 1950s and 1960s brought significant advancements in media technology that revolutionized how the public consumed and engaged with racing.

Print Media and Motor Racing Magazines: Magazines played a pivotal role in chronicling the thrills and tribulations of motorsport. Publications like *Racing Car News*, *Autosport*, and *Road & Track* provided in-depth coverage of races, driver profiles, and technological developments. These magazines not only informed enthusiasts but also attracted new fans by showcasing the excitement and glamour of the sport. High-quality photography and detailed articles brought the drama of the racetrack into the homes of readers, fostering a deeper connection between the audience and the racing world.

Newsreels and Cinematic Coverage: Newsreels, short documentary films shown in cinemas before the main feature, were another crucial medium for motorsport coverage. These visually compelling snippets captured the essence of racing events, featuring highlights, driver interviews, and behind-the-scenes glimpses. The dynamic footage of cars speeding around circuits, smoke billowing from tires, and the intensity of competition captivated audiences, making newsreels a beloved source of entertainment and information about the racing world.

The Advent of Televised Racing: The introduction of television broadcasting marked a seismic shift in motorsport's accessibility and popularity. Live broadcasts of races allowed fans to experience the thrill of racing in real-time, transcending geographical boundaries and making the sport accessible to a broader audience. The first Formula One races to be televised occurred in the early 1950s, but it was the 1960s that truly saw racing becoming a staple of television programming.

Impact of Television on Motorsport: Television brought a new level of immediacy and excitement to motorsport. Viewers could now watch races unfold from the comfort of their living rooms, fostering a more personal and immersive connection with the sport. The visual medium highlighted the speed, skill, and spectacle of racing, enhancing the drama and making races more engaging for the audience. Iconic moments, such as the fierce battles at Monaco or the grueling endurance of Le Mans, were broadcast to millions, solidifying motorsport's place in popular culture.

Televised Narratives and Storytelling: Television also introduced new forms of storytelling and narrative to motorsport. Commentators and broadcasters began to craft narratives around drivers, teams, and rivalries, adding layers of intrigue and personal investment for viewers. This storytelling approach helped to humanize the drivers, transforming them from mere competitors to relatable and admired figures with personal stories and aspirations.

Racing Drivers as Jet-Setting Celebrities

As motorsport gained prominence in the media, drivers themselves became the stars of the show. The combination of their daring exploits on the track and their charismatic personalities off it elevated them to celebrity status, making them icons of style, glamour, and sophistication.

Drivers as Media Personalities: Drivers like Juan Manuel Fangio, Stirling Moss, Jim Clark, and Jackie Stewart became household names, celebrated not only for their racing prowess but also for their personal charm and charisma. These drivers frequently appeared in magazines, newspapers, and later on television, where their interviews and personal stories endeared them to fans. Their presence in the media helped to build a narrative of heroism and glamour around the sport, making racing drivers akin to movie stars and pop icons.

Jet-Setting Lifestyles: The international nature of motorsport meant that top drivers traveled extensively, jet-setting between races across Europe, North America, and beyond. This globetrotting lifestyle contributed to their glamorous image, as they were often seen attending exclusive events, high-end restaurants, and fashion shows. The allure of seeing these drivers in exotic locales added to their celebrity status and the overall glamour associated with motorsport.

Exclusive Parties and Social Circles: Racing events were not just sporting occasions but also social gatherings for the elite. Exclusive parties, gala dinners, and after-race celebrations were integral parts of the racing calendar. Drivers mingled with celebrities, business magnates, and royalty, reinforcing their status as high-profile figures. These social interactions were often covered by the media, further highlighting the glamorous side of racing and attracting fans who admired the lifestyle as much as the sport itself.

Fashion Statements and Public Image: The image of the racing driver extended to fashion and personal style. Drivers were often seen in stylish attire, both on and off the track, setting trends and becoming fashion icons. The sleek helmets, tailored suits, and signature accessories associated with drivers contributed to their sophisticated image, making them role models for style-conscious fans. The emphasis on appearance and personal branding was an early form of what would later become a standard practice in sports celebrity culture.

Influence on Popular Culture: The celebrity status of racing drivers had a significant impact on popular culture. Films like *The Italian Job* and *Grand Prix* drew inspiration from the high-speed, high-stakes world of motorsport, while television shows and advertisements often featured racing stars. The drivers' influence extended beyond the racetrack, shaping trends in music, fashion, and lifestyle, and cementing their place as icons of the era.

The Synergy of Media and Motorsport Glamour

The interplay between media coverage and the burgeoning celebrity culture of racing drivers created a synergistic effect that propelled motorsport into the mainstream. The media not only reported on the races but also helped to craft the narratives and personalities that fans followed with passion. This relationship enhanced the spectacle of racing, making each event not just a competition of speed but a dramatic and engaging story that captivated audiences worldwide.

Marketing and Brand Building: The synergy between media and celebrity drivers also benefited manufacturers and sponsors. Teams could leverage the popularity of their drivers to build their brand and attract sponsors, while sponsors used the drivers' images to promote their products. This mutually beneficial relationship fueled the commercialization of motorsport, providing the financial support necessary for continued innovation and competition.

Global Reach and Fan Engagement: Television and other media platforms expanded the global reach of motorsport, attracting fans from diverse backgrounds and regions. This global fanbase created a vibrant and interconnected community of motorsport enthusiasts who followed races, celebrated their favorite drivers, and participated in the cultural phenomena surrounding the sport.

Enduring Legacy: The legacy of this era's media and celebrity culture is still evident in today's motorsport landscape. Modern racing stars continue to benefit from extensive media coverage and the glamour associated with their profession, maintaining the tradition of drivers as both athletes and cultural icons. The foundations laid during the golden age have ensured that motorsport remains a highly visible and influential part of global popular culture.

Conclusion: The Fusion of Speed and Stardom

The 1950s and 1960s were pivotal in transforming motorsport into a cultural spectacle, blending the thrill of speed with the allure of celebrity and glamour. Media advancements and the emergence of racing drivers as global icons created a rich tapestry of narratives and personalities that captivated audiences and expanded the sport's reach. This fusion of speed and stardom not only enhanced the appeal of motorsport but also set the stage for its continued evolution as a mainstream and culturally significant phenomenon.

As we continue to explore the golden age of motorsport, the role of media and celebrity culture remains a central theme, illustrating how the sport's visibility and glamour contributed to its enduring legacy. The drivers who became legends, the media that broadcast their exploits, and the glamorous lifestyle that surrounded them all played integral roles in shaping the image of motorsport as a thrilling, sophisticated, and highly admired pursuit.

15. Media, Glamour, and Celebrity Culture

The golden age of motorsport was not only a period of intense competition and technological innovation but also an era where the sport intertwined with broader cultural trends, particularly in media and celebrity culture. The 1950s and 1960s saw motorsport transition from a niche passion to a mainstream spectacle, driven by the proliferation of media coverage and the emergence of racing drivers as glamorous, jet-setting celebrities. This chapter explores how magazines, newsreels, and the advent of televised racing expanded the sport's audience, and how drivers became icons of style and sophistication, shaping the public's perception of motorsport.

Magazines, Newsreels, and the Birth of Televised Racing

Before the age of television, motorsport's reach was primarily limited to those who could attend races in person or follow them through print media and newsreels. However, the 1950s and 1960s brought significant advancements in media technology that revolutionized how the public consumed and engaged with racing.

Print Media and Motor Racing Magazines: Magazines played a pivotal role in chronicling the thrills and tribulations of motorsport. Publications like *Racing Car News*, *Autosport*, and *Road & Track* provided in-depth coverage of races, driver profiles, and technological developments. These magazines not only informed enthusiasts but also attracted new fans by showcasing the excitement and glamour of the sport. High-quality photography and detailed articles brought the drama of the racetrack into the homes of readers, fostering a deeper connection between the audience and the racing world.

Newsreels and Cinematic Coverage: Newsreels, short documentary films shown in cinemas before the main feature, were another crucial medium for motorsport coverage. These visually compelling snippets captured the essence of racing events, featuring highlights, driver interviews, and behind-the-scenes glimpses. The dynamic footage of cars speeding around circuits, smoke billowing from tires, and the intensity of competition captivated audiences, making newsreels a beloved source of entertainment and information about the racing world.

The Advent of Televised Racing: The introduction of television broadcasting marked a seismic shift in motorsport's accessibility and popularity. Live broadcasts of races allowed fans to experience the thrill of racing in real-time, transcending geographical boundaries and making the sport accessible to a broader audience. The first Formula One races to be televised occurred in the early 1950s, but it was the 1960s that truly saw racing becoming a staple of television programming.

Impact of Television on Motorsport: Television brought a new level of immediacy and excitement to motorsport. Viewers could now watch races unfold from the comfort of their living rooms, fostering a more personal and immersive connection with the sport. The visual medium highlighted the speed, skill, and spectacle of racing, enhancing the drama and making races more engaging for the audience. Iconic moments, such as the fierce battles at Monaco or the grueling endurance of Le Mans, were broadcast to millions, solidifying motorsport's place in popular culture.

Televised Narratives and Storytelling: Television also introduced new forms of storytelling and narrative to motorsport. Commentators and broadcasters began to craft narratives around drivers, teams, and rivalries, adding layers of intrigue and personal investment for viewers. This storytelling approach helped to humanize the drivers, transforming them from mere competitors to relatable and admired figures with personal stories and aspirations.

Racing Drivers as Jet-Setting Celebrities

As motorsport gained prominence in the media, drivers themselves became the stars of the show. The combination of their daring exploits on the track and their charismatic personalities off it elevated them to celebrity status, making them icons of style, glamour, and sophistication.

Drivers as Media Personalities: Drivers like Juan Manuel Fangio, Stirling Moss, Jim Clark, and Jackie Stewart became household names, celebrated not only for their racing prowess but also for their personal charm and charisma. These drivers frequently appeared in magazines, newspapers, and later on television, where their interviews and personal stories endeared them to fans. Their presence in the media helped to build a narrative of heroism and glamour around the sport, making racing drivers akin to movie stars and pop icons.

Jet-Setting Lifestyles: The international nature of motorsport meant that top drivers traveled extensively, jet-setting between races across Europe, North America, and beyond. This globetrotting lifestyle contributed to their glamorous image, as they were often seen attending exclusive events, high-end restaurants, and fashion shows. The allure of seeing these drivers in exotic locales added to their celebrity status and the overall glamour associated with motorsport.

Exclusive Parties and Social Circles: Racing events were not just sporting occasions but also social gatherings for the elite. Exclusive parties, gala dinners, and after-race celebrations were integral parts of the racing calendar. Drivers mingled with celebrities, business magnates, and royalty, reinforcing their status as high-profile figures. These social interactions were often covered by the media, further highlighting the glamorous side of racing and attracting fans who admired the lifestyle as much as the sport itself.

Fashion Statements and Public Image: The image of the racing driver extended to fashion and personal style. Drivers were often seen in stylish attire, both on and off the track, setting trends and becoming fashion icons. The sleek helmets, tailored suits, and signature accessories associated with drivers contributed to their sophisticated image, making them role models for style-conscious fans. The emphasis on appearance and personal branding was an early form of what would later become a standard practice in sports celebrity culture.

Influence on Popular Culture: The celebrity status of racing drivers had a significant impact on popular culture. Films like *The Italian Job* and *Grand Prix* drew inspiration from the high-speed, high-stakes world of motorsport, while television shows and advertisements often featured racing stars. The drivers' influence extended beyond the racetrack, shaping trends in music, fashion, and lifestyle, and cementing their place as icons of the era.

The Synergy of Media and Motorsport Glamour

The interplay between media coverage and the burgeoning celebrity culture of racing drivers created a synergistic effect that propelled motorsport into the mainstream. The media not only reported on the races but also helped to craft the narratives and personalities that fans followed with passion. This relationship enhanced the spectacle of racing, making each event not just a competition of speed but a dramatic and engaging story that captivated audiences worldwide.

Marketing and Brand Building: The synergy between media and celebrity drivers also benefited manufacturers and sponsors. Teams could leverage the popularity of their drivers to build their brand and attract sponsors, while sponsors used the drivers' images to promote their products. This mutually beneficial relationship fueled the commercialization of motorsport, providing the financial support necessary for continued innovation and competition.

Global Reach and Fan Engagement: Television and other media platforms expanded the global reach of motorsport, attracting fans from diverse backgrounds and regions. This global fanbase created a vibrant and interconnected community of motorsport enthusiasts who followed races, celebrated their favorite drivers, and participated in the cultural phenomena surrounding the sport.

Enduring Legacy: The legacy of this era's media and celebrity culture is still evident in today's motorsport landscape. Modern racing stars continue to benefit from extensive media coverage and the glamour associated with their profession, maintaining the tradition of drivers as both athletes and cultural icons. The foundations laid during the golden age have ensured that motorsport remains a highly visible and influential part of global popular culture.

Conclusion: The Fusion of Speed and Stardom

The 1950s and 1960s were pivotal in transforming motorsport into a cultural spectacle, blending the thrill of speed with the allure of celebrity and glamour. Media advancements and the emergence of racing drivers as global icons created a rich tapestry of narratives and personalities that captivated audiences and expanded the sport's reach. This fusion of speed and stardom not only enhanced the appeal of motorsport but also set the stage for its continued evolution as a mainstream and culturally significant phenomenon.

As we continue to explore the golden age of motorsport, the role of media and celebrity culture remains a central theme, illustrating how the sport's visibility and glamour contributed to its enduring legacy. The drivers who became legends, the media that broadcast their exploits, and the glamorous lifestyle that surrounded them all played integral roles in shaping the image of motorsport as a thrilling, sophisticated, and highly admired pursuit.

17. Underrepresented Stories: Women and Minorities in Racing

While the golden age of motorsport in the 1950s and 1960s was characterized by exhilarating races, legendary drivers, and groundbreaking technological advancements, it was also a time of significant exclusion and underrepresentation for women and minorities. Despite these challenges, a few trailblazers emerged, breaking barriers and paving the way for future generations. This chapter explores the limited yet notable participation of women like Maria Teresa de Filippis in Formula One, the cultural and societal barriers they faced, and the slow, often arduous progress toward broader representation in the sport.

Maria Teresa de Filippis: Pioneering Women in Formula One

Maria Teresa de Filippis stands out as a pioneering figure in the history of Formula One racing. Born on November 24, 1926, in Rome, Italy, de Filippis became the first woman to compete in a Formula One World Championship race, marking a significant milestone in a sport overwhelmingly dominated by men.

Early Beginnings and Entry into Motorsport: De Filippis' interest in racing began in her youth, influenced by her father's involvement in the automotive industry. She started her racing career in Italy, participating in various local and national events. Her determination and skill quickly garnered attention, leading her to compete in more prestigious races. In 1958, de Filippis made her Formula One debut at the Belgian Grand Prix, driving a privately entered

Maserati 250F for the Scuderia Centro Sud team.

Racing Career in Formula One: Despite her historic entry, de Filippis faced numerous challenges in Formula One. The competition was fierce, and the cars were often less forgiving for less experienced drivers. Over the course of her career, she participated in five World Championship Grands Prix, scoring a total of three championship points. Her best finish was 8th place at the 1958 Belgian Grand Prix, a respectable result given the circumstances. De Filippis also competed in various non-championship races, showcasing her talent and resilience.

Legacy and Impact: Maria Teresa de Filippis' participation in Formula One was groundbreaking, demonstrating that women could compete at the highest levels of motorsport. Her legacy is a testament to her courage and passion, inspiring future generations of female racers. Although she did not achieve the same level of success as her male counterparts, her presence in Formula One challenged prevailing stereotypes and opened doors for greater gender diversity in racing.

Cultural Barriers and Societal Attitudes

The participation of women and minorities in motorsport during the 1950s and 1960s was hindered by a myriad of cultural and societal barriers. These obstacles were deeply ingrained in the fabric of the sport and reflected broader societal norms and prejudices of the time.

Gender Stereotypes and Expectations: Motorsport was, and to a large extent remains, perceived as a male-dominated field, associated with physical strength, technical knowledge, and aggressive competitiveness—traits traditionally attributed to men. Women who aspired to compete in racing were often met with skepticism and resistance, both from within the racing community and society at large. The prevailing belief was that women lacked the necessary physical and mental attributes to handle the rigors of high-speed racing.

Limited Access and Opportunities: Opportunities for women and minorities in motorsport were severely limited. Access to racing licenses, funding, and competitive machinery was often restricted to men. Privateers like Maria Teresa de Filippis had to rely on personal wealth, sponsorships, or the support of small teams to compete, as major manufacturers and factory teams were reluctant to invest in female drivers. This lack of institutional support made it exceedingly difficult for women and minorities to break into the sport.

Racism and Discrimination: Minority drivers also faced significant challenges due to racism and discrimination. The motorsport community, predominantly European and American, was not particularly welcoming to drivers from diverse racial and ethnic backgrounds. Racial prejudices limited their opportunities to compete, receive sponsorship, and gain recognition, further marginalizing their presence in the sport.

Media Representation and Public Perception: The media portrayal of women and minority drivers often reinforced stereotypes and failed to acknowledge their achievements.

Coverage was sporadic and frequently focused on the novelty of their participation rather than their skill and accomplishments. This lack of positive representation contributed to the perception that motorsport was an unwelcoming environment for underrepresented groups.

Trailblazers and Their Contributions

Despite these barriers, a handful of women and minority drivers made significant strides in motorsport, challenging the status quo and inspiring future generations.

Lella Lombardi: Following Maria Teresa de Filippis, Lella Lombardi became another notable female driver in Formula One. Born in 1941 in Italy, Lombardi competed in 17 World Championship Grands Prix between 1974 and 1976. She remains the only woman to have scored points in a Formula One race, achieving a half-point finish at the 1975 Spanish Grand Prix. Lombardi's perseverance and success further demonstrated the potential for women in motorsport, even in an era when opportunities were scarce.

Minority Drivers: While the participation of minority drivers in Formula One during this period was minimal, some individuals made attempts to enter the sport. Drivers like Kenny Bräck from Sweden, although emerging in later decades, benefited from the groundwork laid by earlier pioneers. Their stories highlight the ongoing struggle for representation and the slow progress toward inclusivity in motorsport.

Role Models and Mentors: Trailblazers like de Filippis and Lombardi served as role models and mentors for aspiring female drivers, fostering a sense of possibility and encouraging broader participation. Their presence in the sport helped to slowly shift perceptions, demonstrating that skill and determination could overcome societal barriers.

Slow Progress Toward Broader Representation

The path toward broader representation of women and minorities in motorsport was, and continues to be, slow and fraught with challenges. However, the efforts of early pioneers laid the foundation for future advancements.

Incremental Changes in Regulations: Gradually, changes in regulations and attitudes began to support greater inclusivity. Organizations like the Fédération Internationale de l'Automobile (FIA) started to implement policies aimed at increasing diversity, although progress was slow and often met with resistance from traditionalist factions within the sport.

Rise of Supportive Organizations: The establishment of organizations dedicated to supporting women and minority drivers played a crucial role in fostering greater representation. Initiatives like the Women in Motorsport Commission and various scholarships and training programs provided essential resources and encouragement for underrepresented groups to pursue careers in racing.

Cultural Shifts and Awareness: As societal attitudes evolved, so did the perception of motorsport. The increasing awareness of the need for diversity and inclusion led to more support for female and minority drivers, both from within the racing community and from the public. This cultural shift was instrumental in creating a more welcoming environment for all participants.

Legacy and Continued Efforts: The legacy of early female and minority drivers continues to inspire current and future generations. Efforts to promote diversity in motorsport have gained momentum, with more initiatives aimed at breaking down barriers and providing opportunities for underrepresented groups. The stories of pioneers like Maria Teresa de Filippis and Lella Lombardi serve as enduring reminders of the progress made and the work that still lies ahead.

Conclusion: Acknowledging the Pioneers and Moving Forward

The stories of women and minorities in motorsport during the 1950s and 1960s are emblematic of the broader struggles for equality and representation in society. Despite facing significant cultural and institutional barriers, pioneers like Maria Teresa de Filippis and Lella Lombardi made invaluable contributions to the sport, challenging stereotypes and opening doors for future generations.

Their perseverance and achievements highlight the resilience and passion required to break into a male-dominated field, serving as powerful inspirations for aspiring drivers from all backgrounds. While the progress toward broader representation has been slow, the foundations laid by these early trailblazers have been instrumental in fostering a more inclusive and diverse motorsport landscape.

As motorsport continues to evolve, the legacy of these pioneers reminds us of the importance of diversity and the ongoing need to support and celebrate the achievements of all participants. By acknowledging and learning from the underrepresented stories of the past, the sport can move forward toward a future where motorsport is truly inclusive, reflecting the rich diversity of its global fanbase and participant community.

18. Tuning and Mechanics: The Unsung Heroes of the Paddock

Behind every roaring engine and every breathtaking maneuver on the track stood a dedicated team of mechanics, engineers, and team managers whose expertise and tireless efforts ensured that racing cars performed at their peak. While drivers often basked in the limelight, it was these unsung heroes who refined setups, optimized engines, and kept the machines running under the most demanding conditions. This chapter delves into the crucial roles played by these skilled artisans, highlighting their innovations and contributions that were pivotal to the successes of the golden age of motorsport.

The Backbone of Racing: Mechanics and Their Craft

Mechanics were the lifeblood of racing teams, responsible for the intricate maintenance and rapid repairs that kept cars competitive throughout grueling races. Their hands-on work behind the scenes was essential for managing the relentless wear and tear that high-speed racing imposed on vehicles.

Precision Maintenance and Repairs: In an era before computerized diagnostics, mechanics relied on their deep understanding of automotive systems and their ability to perform precise manual adjustments. They meticulously checked and adjusted engine components, suspension setups, and braking systems to ensure optimal performance. During races, mechanics worked swiftly to address any mechanical issues, often under extreme time pressure, to minimize downtime and keep their drivers on the track.

Custom Modifications and Enhancements: Mechanics also played a key role in customizing and enhancing racing cars. They collaborated closely with engineers to implement modifications that could provide competitive advantages, such as adjusting gear ratios for better acceleration or modifying suspension settings to improve handling on specific circuits. Their ability to translate engineering designs into practical applications was crucial for adapting cars to the unique demands of each race.

Notable Mechanics: One such mechanic was Mauro Forghieri, who worked with Ferrari and later with other teams. Forghieri was instrumental in developing Ferrari's engine performance, contributing to the company's successes in both Formula One and endurance racing. His technical prowess and innovative approach exemplified the critical role mechanics played in advancing racing technology.

Engineering Excellence: Designing the Perfect Race Car

Engineers were the visionaries who transformed raw mechanical components into sophisticated racing machines. Their expertise in design, aerodynamics, and materials science drove the technological advancements that defined the golden age of motorsport.

Aerodynamic Innovations: Engineers like Maurice Philippe of Lotus pioneered aerodynamic designs that significantly improved car performance. Philippe's work on the Lotus 25, the first Formula One car to feature a monocoque chassis, demonstrated how aerodynamics could enhance stability and speed. By carefully shaping the bodywork to reduce drag and increase downforce, engineers enabled cars to navigate corners more efficiently and maintain higher speeds on straights.

Engine Optimization: Engineers focused on extracting maximum performance from engines through meticulous tuning and innovative design. The development of lightweight, high-revving engines was a priority, with engineers experimenting with different configurations to achieve the best balance between power and reliability. Ferrari's Carlo Chiti, for example, was renowned for his expertise in engine tuning, contributing to the creation of some of the most powerful and reliable engines in racing history.

Suspension and Chassis Design: Advancements in suspension systems and chassis design were critical for improving handling and driver control. Engineers like Colin Chapman of Lotus emphasized lightweight construction and agile handling, which became hallmarks of British racing success. The introduction of double wishbone suspensions and adjustable dampers allowed for greater customization of car setups, enabling teams to fine-tune their vehicles for specific tracks and conditions.

Strategic Minds: Team Managers and Their Leadership

Team managers were the orchestrators who coordinated the various elements of a racing team, ensuring that mechanics, engineers, and drivers worked in harmony to achieve success. Their strategic decisions and leadership were essential for navigating the complexities of motorsport competition.

Race Strategy and Logistics: Managers devised race strategies that accounted for variables such as track conditions, weather, and competitor behavior. They made critical decisions regarding pit stops, tire changes, and fuel management, often in real-time as races unfolded. Effective logistics management ensured that teams arrived at races prepared, with cars meticulously maintained and all necessary equipment on hand.

Coordination and Communication: Team managers facilitated clear and efficient communication between drivers, mechanics, and engineers. They ensured that feedback from drivers about car performance was accurately conveyed to engineers, enabling timely adjustments and improvements. This seamless coordination was vital for maintaining peak performance throughout the race.

Leadership and Motivation: Beyond technical expertise, managers provided the leadership and motivation that kept teams focused and driven. They fostered a collaborative environment where each team member felt valued and empowered to contribute their best efforts. Legendary team managers like Enzo Ferrari exemplified this role, blending passion with pragmatism to lead their teams to numerous victories.

Innovative Breakthroughs: Pioneering Technologies and Techniques

The relentless pursuit of performance led mechanics and engineers to develop groundbreaking technologies and techniques that pushed the boundaries of what was possible in motorsport.

Disc Brakes and Improved Stopping Power: The adoption of disc brakes was a significant technological advancement that enhanced car safety and performance. Pioneered by teams like Jaguar, disc brakes provided superior stopping power and reduced brake fade during intense racing conditions. Mechanics played a crucial role in installing and maintaining these advanced braking systems, ensuring their reliability and effectiveness on the track.

Monocoque Chassis Construction: The shift from spaceframe to monocoque chassis construction revolutionized racing car design. Engineers like Colin Chapman introduced the monocoque chassis with the Lotus 25, which offered greater rigidity and reduced weight compared to traditional designs. This innovation not only improved handling and performance but also laid the foundation for modern racing car construction.

Hydraulic Systems and Electronics: The introduction of hydraulic systems for clutch operation and brake actuation marked another leap forward in racing technology. While still rudimentary compared to today's standards, these systems provided more precise control and responsiveness. Engineers began experimenting with electronic components, laying the groundwork for the sophisticated telemetry and data acquisition systems that would emerge in later decades.

Collaborative Efforts: The Synergy Between Drivers and Technical Teams

Successful racing was the result of a symbiotic relationship between drivers and their technical teams. Drivers provided invaluable feedback on car performance, allowing mechanics and engineers to make informed adjustments and improvements.

Driver Feedback and Car Development: Drivers like Jim Clark and Stirling Moss were not only exceptional talents behind the wheel but also keen observers of car behavior. Their insights into handling, acceleration, and braking informed the technical teams' efforts to refine car setups and enhance performance. This collaborative approach ensured that cars were not only fast but also tailored to each driver's unique style and preferences.

Continuous Improvement and Innovation: The dynamic environment of racing demanded continuous improvement and innovation. Technical teams were in a constant state of experimentation, testing new components and configurations to gain a competitive edge. This relentless drive for improvement fostered a culture of innovation, where successful ideas were rapidly implemented and failures served as lessons for future developments.

Notable Figures: Engineers and Mechanics Who Made a Difference

Several individuals stand out for their exceptional contributions to racing during this era, driving technological advancements and team successes through their expertise and dedication.

Maurice Philippe (Lotus): As Lotus's chief designer, Maurice Philippe was instrumental in developing the monocoque chassis and pioneering aerodynamic designs. His work on the Lotus 25 and subsequent models established Lotus as a leader in Formula One innovation, directly contributing to the team's competitive success.

Carlo Chiti (Ferrari and Tec-Mec): Carlo Chiti was a key engineer at Ferrari, responsible for developing powerful and reliable engines that powered the team's victories in both Formula One and endurance racing. His technical expertise and innovative approach were pivotal in maintaining Ferrari's competitive edge.

Mauro Forghieri (Ferrari and Ferrari's Technical Team): Mauro Forghieri played a significant role in Ferrari's engineering team, overseeing the development of advanced engine and chassis designs. His contributions were essential to Ferrari's successes in the 1960s, including their victories at Le Mans and in Formula One.

Colin Chapman (Lotus): Beyond his role as a designer, Colin Chapman was a visionary leader who emphasized lightweight construction and aerodynamic efficiency. His philosophy of "adding lightness" drove numerous innovations that set Lotus apart from its competitors and influenced the broader motorsport engineering landscape.

John Cooper (Cooper Car Company): John Cooper's expertise in mid-engine car design revolutionized Formula One racing. His designs emphasized balanced weight distribution and superior handling, leading to multiple championship victories and inspiring other British teams to adopt similar layouts.

Conclusion: Celebrating the Unsung Heroes

The golden age of motorsport was defined not only by the daring exploits of its drivers but also by the unwavering dedication and ingenuity of its mechanics, engineers, and team managers. These unsung heroes worked tirelessly behind the scenes, turning raw talent and passion into technological marvels and race-winning strategies. Their contributions were indispensable to the sport's evolution, fostering an environment where innovation and collaboration thrived alongside the thrill of competition.

As motorsport continued to grow and professionalize, the roles of mechanics and engineers became increasingly specialized and integral to team success. The legacy of these pioneers is evident in the sophisticated, high-performance racing machines and the strategic, well-coordinated teams that dominate the sport today. By celebrating the achievements of these unsung heroes, we acknowledge the vital foundation they built, ensuring that the golden age of speed was not only a time of heroic drivers and legendary races but also an era of remarkable engineering excellence and collaborative triumph.

19. Shifts in Driving Ethos and Professionalism

The golden age of motorsport was not only a period of technological marvels and legendary rivalries but also a transformative era that witnessed profound changes in the ethos and professionalism of racing drivers. During the 1950s and 1960s, the sport evolved from a daring spectacle dominated by daredevil attitudes to a more methodical, data-informed discipline. Simultaneously, drivers began to assert their rights, demanding better working conditions, comprehensive insurance, and contractual security. These shifts reflected the sport's maturation, balancing the inherent risks of racing with a growing emphasis on driver welfare and strategic excellence.

From Daredevil Attitudes to Methodical, Data-Informed Approaches

In the early days of motorsport, drivers were often seen as fearless daredevils, driven by sheer adrenaline and a love for speed. The 1950s and early 1960s epitomized this archetype, with drivers like Stirling Moss, Jim Clark, and Richie Ginther embodying the reckless bravery that defined the era. Races were not only tests of speed but also of courage, as drivers navigated perilous circuits with minimal safety measures.

Evolution of Driving Techniques: As the sport progressed, a shift occurred towards more strategic and calculated driving techniques. The increasing complexity of race cars, combined with advancements in engineering, necessitated a deeper understanding of vehicle dynamics and race strategy. Drivers began to adopt a more analytical approach, utilizing data to optimize their performance. This transition was facilitated by the introduction of telemetry systems and more sophisticated data collection methods, allowing drivers and teams to make informed decisions based on real-time information.

Influence of Technology and Engineering: The integration of technology into racing played a pivotal role in this shift. Engineers like Colin Chapman of Lotus emphasized the importance of car setup and aerodynamics, pushing drivers to work closely with their technical teams. The development of monocoque chassis, advanced suspension systems, and aerodynamic enhancements required drivers to possess a nuanced understanding of their vehicles. This collaboration between driver and engineer fostered a more methodical approach to racing, where precision and strategy became as important as raw speed.

Strategic Racing and Team Coordination: The rise of team-based strategies also contributed to the evolution of driving ethos. Unlike the individualistic approach of earlier decades, modern racing increasingly involved coordinated team efforts, including pit stop strategies, tire management, and fuel conservation. Drivers like Jack Brabham and Bruce McLaren excelled not only for their driving skills but also for their ability to work within a team framework, balancing personal ambition with collective goals. This shift emphasized the importance of teamwork and strategic planning, moving the sport away from the lone hero narrative to a more collaborative and organized discipline.

Drivers Demanding Better Conditions, Insurance, and Contractual Security

As motorsport became more professional, drivers began to recognize the need for improved working conditions, comprehensive insurance, and contractual protections. This era saw the emergence of drivers advocating for their rights and pushing for systemic changes to enhance their safety and job security.

Recognition of Risks and the Need for Safety Measures: The high fatality rates and severe injuries that plagued motorsport in the 1950s and 1960s underscored the urgent need for better safety measures. Drivers like Jackie Stewart became vocal advocates for enhanced safety protocols, campaigning for safer track designs, improved car construction, and the implementation of protective gear. Stewart's relentless pursuit of safety reforms led to significant changes, including the introduction of safer barriers, better medical facilities at tracks, and mandatory fire-resistant suits for drivers.

Insurance and Financial Security: The financial risks associated with racing were immense, with drivers often facing medical bills, loss of income, and the potential loss of their careers due to injuries. During this period, drivers began to demand better insurance coverage to protect themselves against these risks. The establishment of comprehensive insurance policies became a priority, ensuring that drivers were financially safeguarded in the event of accidents. This development was crucial in transitioning racing from a perilous hobby to a viable professional career.

Contractual Protections and Labor Rights: As the sport matured, drivers sought greater control over their careers and better contractual terms. The formation of drivers' unions and associations began to take shape, advocating for fair wages, working conditions, and contractual rights. Drivers like Phil Hill and Dan Gurney were instrumental in negotiating better terms with teams and manufacturers, ensuring that their contributions were recognized and rewarded appropriately. These efforts laid the groundwork for the modern contractual frameworks that govern driver-team relationships today.

Professionalization and Structured Career Paths: The increasing demands for professionalism also led to the development of more structured career paths for drivers. Formal training programs, driver development initiatives, and support systems were established to nurture talent and ensure that drivers were equipped with the necessary skills and knowledge to compete safely and effectively. This professionalization helped to elevate the sport, attracting a new generation of drivers who approached racing with a combination of passion and professionalism.

Balancing Tradition and Modernity

The shifts in driving ethos and professionalism during the golden age of motorsport represented a delicate balance between preserving the sport's adventurous spirit and embracing the necessities of modern competition. While the daredevil attitudes that characterized early racing remained an integral part of its allure, the adoption of methodical, data-informed approaches and the push for better driver protections signified a maturation that was essential for the sport's sustainability.

Preservation of the Racing Spirit: Despite the move towards greater professionalism, the inherent thrill and danger of motorsport continued to attract passionate drivers and fans. The legacy of drivers who embodied both bravery and skill, such as Stirling Moss and Jim Clark, remained a source of inspiration, highlighting that the essence of racing was still rooted in the pursuit of speed and excellence.

Integration of Safety and Strategy: The integration of safety measures and strategic approaches did not diminish the excitement of racing; rather, it enhanced it by allowing drivers to push the limits of their performance within a safer and more controlled environment. This harmony between safety and speed ensured that the sport could evolve without losing its core appeal, maintaining a dynamic and engaging spectacle for generations of fans.

Conclusion: A New Era of Professionalism and Safety

The 1950s and 1960s were pivotal in transforming motorsport from a perilous adventure into a more structured and professional discipline. The shift from daredevil attitudes to methodical, data-informed approaches marked a significant evolution in driving ethos, driven by advancements in technology and a deeper understanding of racing dynamics. Concurrently, drivers' demands for better conditions, insurance, and contractual security underscored the sport's maturation, fostering an environment where safety and professionalism became paramount.

These changes not only enhanced the performance and competitiveness of racing but also ensured the well-being and sustainability of its participants. The legacy of this era is evident in today's motorsport landscape, where the balance between speed and safety continues to shape the sport's evolution. As motorsport moved forward, the lessons learned and the strides made in professionalism and driver protections laid the foundation for a safer, more organized, and ultimately more thrilling racing experience.

20. The Winds of Change: Late 1960s Transitions

As the 1960s drew to a close, motorsport found itself at a pivotal juncture. The decade had been marked by rapid technological advancements, intense rivalries, and significant shifts in the sport's cultural and economic landscape. However, it was also a period of increasing recognition of the inherent dangers of racing, leading to a push for enhanced safety measures and regulatory reforms. Additionally, the emergence of corporate sponsorships began to reshape the financial and operational aspects of racing teams. This chapter explores the multifaceted transitions that defined the late 1960s in motorsport, focusing on the influence of safety advocates like Jackie Stewart, the implementation of new technical regulations, the modernization or abandonment of beloved tracks, and the rise of corporate backing.

The Influence of Safety Advocates Like Jackie Stewart

Jackie Stewart, a Scottish Formula One driver, emerged as a leading voice for safety in motorsport during the late 1960s. His advocacy played a crucial role in transforming the sport's approach to safety, influencing both regulatory bodies and track designers to prioritize driver protection.

Stewart's Advocacy and Campaigns: By the late 1960s, the high fatality rates in Formula One had become a growing concern. Stewart, who had experienced personal losses on the track, became a passionate advocate for improved safety standards. He actively lobbied for better track designs, enhanced driver equipment, and stricter safety regulations. Stewart's efforts were instrumental in raising awareness about the dangers of racing and the urgent need for reforms.

Impact on Safety Regulations: Stewart's advocacy led to significant changes in Formula One regulations. The Fédération Internationale de l'Automobile (FIA) began to implement stricter safety measures, including the introduction of larger run-off areas, better crash barriers, and improvements in circuit infrastructure. The implementation of fire-resistant suits, safer helmets, and the mandatory use of seat belts also stemmed from the growing emphasis on driver safety.

Legacy of Jackie Stewart: Stewart's influence extended beyond immediate safety improvements. He continued to champion driver safety throughout his career and beyond, contributing to the establishment of the Drivers' Safety Committee in 1969. His persistent efforts laid the groundwork for the comprehensive safety standards that would be further developed in subsequent decades, significantly reducing the number of fatalities and severe injuries in the sport.

New Technical Regulations

The late 1960s witnessed a series of technical regulation changes aimed at improving safety, enhancing competition, and controlling costs within motorsport. These regulations not only affected car designs but also influenced team strategies and the overall dynamics of racing competitions.

Engine Regulations and Power Limits: In response to safety concerns and the escalating speeds of Formula One cars, the FIA introduced regulations to limit engine power and displacement. The 1966 season saw the reduction of engine capacities, which aimed to decrease the top speeds and reduce the potential for catastrophic crashes. These changes necessitated significant adjustments in car design, prompting engineers to focus more on aerodynamics and handling rather than sheer power.

Chassis and Structural Safety: Regulations were also introduced to enhance the structural integrity of racing cars. The use of stronger, crash-resistant materials became mandatory, and the design of chassis was scrutinized to ensure better protection for drivers in the event of a collision. The move towards monocoque chassis construction, pioneered by teams like Lotus, was accelerated by these safety-focused regulations.

Aerodynamic Restrictions: To control the aerodynamic advancements that were contributing to increasing speeds, the FIA imposed restrictions on wing sizes and other aerodynamic features. These limitations aimed to prevent cars from generating excessive downforce, which could lead to unstable handling at high speeds. Teams had to innovate within these constraints, leading to more balanced and manageable car designs.

Impact on Competition: These technical regulations had a profound impact on the competitive landscape of Formula One. Teams that could adapt quickly to the new rules gained an advantage, while those reliant on outdated technologies struggled to keep pace. The emphasis shifted towards engineering ingenuity and strategic car development, fostering a more technically diverse and competitive field.

Modernization or Abandonment of Beloved Tracks

As safety became a paramount concern, several iconic racing circuits underwent significant modifications or were retired altogether. The transformation of these tracks reflected the evolving priorities of the motorsport community, balancing tradition with the necessity of enhanced safety measures.

Modernization Efforts: Tracks like the Nürburgring and Spa-Francorchamps, known for their challenging and perilous layouts, were subject to extensive safety overhauls. This included widening of track sections, installation of better barriers, and the addition of safety run-offs to reduce the risk of fatal accidents. These modifications aimed to preserve the historical significance of these circuits while making them safer for drivers and spectators.

Abandonment of Hazardous Tracks: Some circuits, deemed too dangerous even after attempted safety enhancements, were retired from the Formula One calendar. For instance, the original configuration of the Nürburgring Nordschleife was increasingly viewed as too risky, leading to the construction of the modern Nürburgring GP-Strecke, which featured a more controlled and safer layout. Similarly, certain sections of tracks that could not be adequately upgraded were abandoned, ensuring that only the safest venues remained active.

New Safe Venues: The push for safety also led to the development of new, purpose-built circuits designed with modern safety standards in mind. Tracks like the Circuit de Monaco underwent redesigns to enhance safety while maintaining their unique characteristics. The establishment of newer venues with state-of-the-art safety features allowed Formula One to continue expanding its global reach without compromising on driver protection.

Preservation of Racing Heritage: While some tracks were modernized or abandoned, efforts were made to preserve the heritage and legacy of the classic circuits. Museums, historic race events, and preservation societies worked to maintain the cultural and historical significance of these venues, ensuring that the stories and memories associated with them remained accessible to future generations.

The Emergence of Corporate Backing

The late 1960s also saw the rise of corporate sponsorships and financial investments from multinational companies, fundamentally altering the economic landscape of motorsport. This shift brought about increased professionalism, higher operational costs, and greater global visibility for the sport.

Rise of Corporate Sponsorships: As racing teams sought additional funding to compete with well-financed factory teams, corporate sponsorships became increasingly important. Brands like Shell, Marlboro, and Ford began to invest heavily in racing, leveraging the sport's global appeal to enhance their brand visibility and market reach. These sponsorships provided essential financial support, enabling teams to invest in better technology, hire top-tier drivers, and expand their operations internationally.

Impact on Team Operations: Corporate backing introduced a new level of professionalism within racing teams. With substantial financial resources, teams could afford advanced research and development, cutting-edge technology, and comprehensive training programs for drivers and staff. This financial influx also allowed for more extensive logistical support, including international travel, sophisticated marketing strategies, and the establishment of global racing hubs.

Enhanced Marketing and Global Reach: Corporate sponsorships facilitated the global expansion of motorsport by providing the necessary funding for international events and marketing campaigns. Brands utilized racing as a platform to reach diverse markets, enhancing the sport's global appeal and attracting a broader audience. The integration of branded liveries and advertisements on cars, driver uniforms, and team facilities also contributed to the commercialization and mainstream acceptance of motorsport.

Influence on Competition and Innovation: The influx of corporate funding spurred increased competition among teams, as sponsors sought to associate their brands with success and innovation. This competition drove teams to push the boundaries of technology and performance, fostering an environment of continuous improvement and creative problem-solving. Corporate investments also facilitated the development of specialized roles within teams, such as dedicated marketing managers and financial analysts, further professionalizing the sport.

Legacy of Corporate Backing: The emergence of corporate backing in the late 1960s set the stage for the highly commercialized and globally interconnected motorsport industry seen today. The financial stability provided by sponsors enabled sustained technological advancements and the professionalization of teams, ensuring that motorsport remained at the forefront of sporting innovation and global entertainment.

Conclusion: Navigating a New Era of Safety and Professionalism

The late 1960s were a time of profound transformation in motorsport, marked by a concerted effort to enhance safety, adapt to new technical regulations, modernize or retire historic tracks, and embrace corporate sponsorships. The influence of safety advocates like Jackie Stewart was instrumental in shifting the sport's priorities towards driver protection and regulatory compliance. Concurrently, the introduction of stringent technical regulations and the modernization of racing venues ensured that motorsport could evolve without sacrificing the thrill and excitement that captivated fans.

The emergence of corporate backing ushered in a new era of professionalism and financial stability, enabling teams to pursue technological excellence and compete on a global scale. These transitions collectively redefined the landscape of motorsport, balancing the preservation of its rich heritage with the demands of modern competition and safety standards.

As motorsport continued to navigate these changes, the foundations laid during the golden age ensured that the sport could sustain its popularity and competitive edge. The legacy of the late 1960s is one of resilience and adaptation, demonstrating how motorsport could honor its past while embracing the innovations and safety measures necessary for its future. This period of transition not only enhanced the sport's safety and professionalism but also solidified its position as a premier global spectacle, setting the stage for the continued evolution and enduring legacy of motorsport.

Epilogue: Legacy of the Golden Age

The golden age of motorsport, spanning the vibrant decades of the 1950s and 1960s, remains a cornerstone in the annals of racing history. This transformative era, marked by daring drivers, groundbreaking engineering, and the burgeoning spectacle of global competition, continues to resonate within modern motorsport culture. As we reflect on the enduring romance of those years, the lessons learned, and the profound influence they exert on today's racing world, it becomes evident that the legacy of the golden age is both a beacon of inspiration and a foundation upon which contemporary motorsport is built.

Enduring Romance and Inspirational Legacy

The allure of the golden age lies in its perfect blend of speed, glamour, and human drama. Races were not merely competitions of horsepower and skill but grand spectacles where technology, courage, and national pride intersected. The images of legendary drivers maneuvering their finely tuned machines through iconic circuits, the roar of engines echoing through lush European landscapes, and the vibrant celebrations of victory capture a romanticized vision of racing that continues to captivate fans today.

This era fostered a mythology around motorsport, elevating drivers to near-mythic status and transforming racing teams into symbols of national and corporate pride. The stories of figures like Juan Manuel Fangio, Stirling Moss, and Maria Teresa de Filippis inspire countless enthusiasts and aspiring drivers, reminding them of the passion and perseverance required to excel in the sport. The golden age's narrative of innovation, resilience, and the relentless pursuit of excellence serves as a timeless source of motivation, encouraging modern teams and drivers to push the boundaries of what is possible.

Lessons Learned: Safety, Professionalism, and Innovation

The 1950s and 1960s were not without their perils. The tragic losses and near-disasters of this period underscored the urgent need for improved safety measures, prompting significant advancements that have saved countless lives and preserved the sport's integrity. The tireless advocacy of safety pioneers like Jackie Stewart led to the implementation of stringent safety regulations, better track designs, and the development of protective gear that have become standard in modern racing. These lessons highlighted the importance of prioritizing driver welfare without sacrificing the thrill and competitive spirit that define motorsport.

Professionalism also took center stage during the golden age. The transition from amateur enthusiasts to highly organized, factory-backed teams transformed racing into a sophisticated, data-driven discipline. This shift emphasized the importance of teamwork, strategic planning, and technological innovation—principles that continue to underpin the success of modern racing teams. The era demonstrated that sustained excellence in motorsport requires not only exceptional driving talent but also meticulous engineering, effective management, and a harmonious collaboration between all team members.

Inspiration for Modern Motorsport Culture

The golden age's influence extends beyond technological and professional advancements to shape the very culture of motorsport today. The integration of media, glamour, and celebrity culture during this period laid the groundwork for how racing is marketed and consumed in the contemporary era. The visibility gained through magazines, newsreels, and the advent of televised races transformed motorsport into a global spectacle, attracting a diverse and passionate fanbase. Modern racing continues to leverage these media platforms to engage audiences, celebrate driver personalities, and promote brand partnerships, echoing the pioneering efforts of the golden age.

Furthermore, the era's spirit of innovation and fearless competition fosters a culture of continuous improvement and technological experimentation in today's motorsport. Teams relentlessly pursue aerodynamic efficiencies, advanced materials, and cutting-edge engineering solutions, inspired by the trailblazing advancements of their predecessors. The balance of heritage and innovation ensures that while racing evolves, it remains deeply connected to its rich historical roots.

Balancing Nostalgia and Reality

While nostalgia for the golden age of motorsport is well-deserved, it is essential to balance this romanticized view with an understanding of the era's harsh realities. The glamour and excitement of the time were often juxtaposed with significant risks and sacrifices, reminding us that progress in motorsport has always been driven by both triumphs and tragedies. Acknowledging the challenges faced by drivers, mechanics, and teams during this period provides a more nuanced appreciation of their achievements and the strides made toward making racing safer and more inclusive.

The golden age also serves as a reminder of the importance of preserving the sport's history while embracing necessary changes. Beloved tracks have been modernized or retired to enhance safety, and the increasing professionalism and commercialization of racing have transformed it into a highly regulated and commercially driven sport. Balancing the reverence for the past with the demands of the present ensures that motorsport honors its heritage while continuing to evolve and thrive in a modern context.

A Foundation for a Diverse and Inclusive Future

The stories of women and minority drivers from the golden age, though few in number, highlight the importance of diversity and inclusion in motorsport. Their pioneering efforts, despite the significant cultural and societal barriers they faced, laid the groundwork for future advancements toward a more inclusive racing environment. Modern initiatives aimed at promoting diversity and supporting underrepresented groups in motorsport are built upon the foundation established by these early trailblazers, ensuring that the sport continues to grow and reflect the diverse global community it serves.

Conclusion: A Timeless Influence

The golden age of motorsport remains a pivotal chapter in the sport's history, embodying a time of unparalleled innovation, fierce competition, and cultural significance. Its legacy is a testament to the enduring romance of racing, the critical lessons learned in safety and professionalism, and the inspirational narratives that continue to shape modern motorsport culture. As we look back on the 1950s and 1960s, we celebrate the achievements and sacrifices of those who defined this era, while also recognizing the ongoing journey toward a safer, more inclusive, and technologically advanced racing world.

The golden age's harmonious blend of speed, technology, and human spirit continues to inspire and guide motorsport today, ensuring that the echoes of those transformative decades resonate through every race, every innovation, and every champion who takes to the track. Balancing nostalgia with an appreciation for progress, the legacy of the golden age endures, affirming that the heart of motorsport lies in its ability to evolve while honoring the passion and ingenuity that have always driven it forward.

Appendix: Photo Gallery

The following photo gallery serves as a visual companion to the narratives and themes explored throughout this book. Each image captures the essence of the golden age of motorsport, highlighting iconic moments, legendary figures, and groundbreaking innovations that defined the 1950s and 1960s. This collection not only commemorates the thrilling history of racing but also honors the individuals and technologies that propelled the sport into its modern era.

1. The Resurgence of Motorsport Post-War

A 1949 Le Mans Race

2. Economic Boom and Engineering Innovations

A bustling automotive factory in the early 1950s

3. The Titans of the Early 1950s

Juan Manuel Fangio alongside his Mercedes-Benz W196

4. Ascendancy of the British and the Mid-Engine Revolution

A Cooper T43 mid-engine car at Silverstone.

5. The New Wave of 1960s Driving Icons

Jim Clark celebrating a victory at the 1965 Indianapolis 500

6. Formula One's Coming of Age

The inaugural 1950 Formula One World Championship race

7. Europe's Legendary Circuits and Classic Grands Prix

The iconic Eau Rouge corner at Spa-Francorchamps.

8. Sports Car Racing and Endurance Battles

The Ferrari 500 TR

9. The American Scene: Indy, USAC, and NASCAR

The front-engined roadsters competing at the Indianapolis 500 in the early 1960s.

10. Cross-Pollination of Ideas: Europe Meets America

The Ford GT40 celebrating its Le Mans victory in 1966

11. Mechanical Marvels: Engineering and Design Breakthroughs

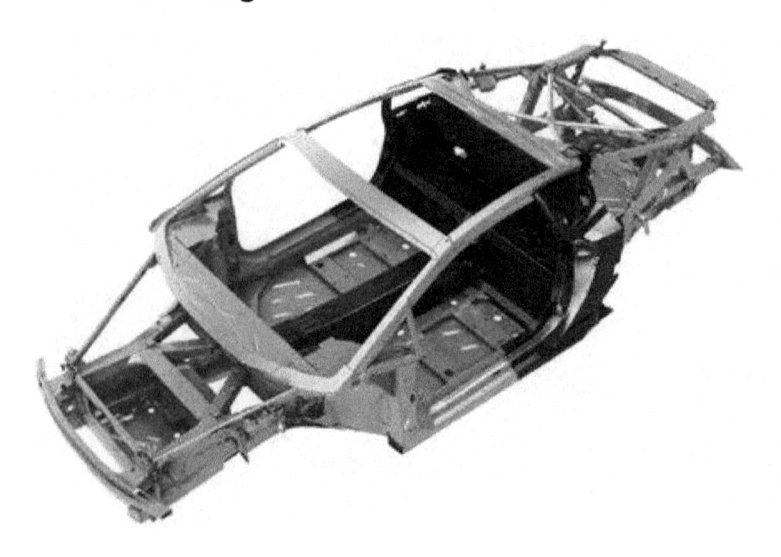

A close-up of a monocoque chassis

12. Safety on the Edge: Dangers and Disasters

Memorial at the 1955 Le Mans circuit.

13. Commercialization and the Start of Sponsorship

A Lotus 25 with the Gold Leaf livery

14. Media, Glamour, and Celebrity Culture

Jackie Stewart - 1969

15. The Role of Privateers and Gentleman Racers

Vinayak: Privateer who held his own against factory teams in tough Safari Rally of yore

16. Underrepresented Stories: Women and Minorities in Racing

Maria Teresa de Filippis at her Maserati during a race weekend.

17. Tuning and Mechanics: The Unsung Heroes of the Paddock

Mechanics working on a Ferrari in the pit lane.

18. Shifts in Driving Ethos and Professionalism

Jackie Stewart discussing car setup with engineers before a race

19. The Winds of Change: Late 1960s Transitions

Modernized Circuit de Monaco with updated safety features

About the Author

Etienne Psaila, an accomplished author with over two decades of experience, has mastered the art of weaving words across various genres. His journey in the literary world has been marked by a diverse array of publications, demonstrating not only his versatility but also his deep understanding of different thematic landscapes. However, it's in the realm of automotive literature that Etienne truly combines his passions, seamlessly blending his enthusiasm for cars with his innate storytelling abilities.

Specializing in automotive and motorcycle books, Etienne brings to life the world of automobiles through his eloquent prose and an array of stunning, high-quality color photographs. His works are a tribute to the industry, capturing its evolution, technological advancements, and the sheer beauty of vehicles in a manner that is both informative and visually captivating.

A proud alumnus of the University of Malta, Etienne's academic background lays a solid foundation for his meticulous research and factual accuracy. His education has not only enriched his writing but has also fueled his career as a dedicated teacher. In the classroom, just as in his writing, Etienne strives to inspire, inform, and ignite a passion for learning.

As a teacher, Etienne harnesses his experience in writing to engage and educate, bringing the same level of dedication and excellence to his students as he does to his readers. His dual role as an educator and author makes him uniquely positioned to understand and convey complex concepts with clarity and ease, whether in the classroom or through the pages of his books.

Through his literary works, Etienne Psaila continues to leave an indelible mark on the world of automotive literature, captivating car enthusiasts and readers alike with his insightful perspectives and compelling narratives.

Visit www.etiennepsaila.com for more.